PILC
THE PURPLE
TWILIGHT

The Story of Canada's
Early Bush Flyers

Philip H. Godsell

FIFTH
HOUSE

Cover painting, "Barrens Pioneer," by Graeme Shaw
Cover and interior design by John Luckhurst / GDL
Interior photographs courtesy The Glenbow Archives, Calgary, Alberta, Canada.

Editor's Note:
The terms used by the author in the 1955 edition have been retained in this edition.

The publisher gratefully acknowledges the support of The Canada Council for the Arts and the Department of Canadian Heritage. We acknowledge the financial support of the Government of Canada through the Book Publishing Industry Development Program for our publishing activities.

THE CANADA COUNCIL | LE CONSEIL DES ARTS
FOR THE ARTS | DU CANADA
SINCE 1957 | DEPUIS 1957

Printed in Canada by Transcontinental Printing.

02 03 04 05 06 / 5 4 3 2 1

National Library of Canada Cataloguing in Publication Data

Godsell, Philip H. (Philip Henry), 1889-1961
        Pilots of the purple twilight

   ISBN 1-894004-98-1

1. Bush flying–Canada, Northern–History. 2. Bush
pilots–Canada–Biography. I. Title.
TL523.G6 2002   629.13'092'271   C2002-911005-X

First published in the United States in 2003.

Fifth House Ltd.
A Fitzhenry & Whiteside Company
1511-1800 4 St. SW
Calgary, Alberta, Canada
T2S 2S5

In the United States:
Fitzhenry & Whiteside
121 Harvard Avenue, Suite 2
Allston, MA 02134

1-800-387-9776
www.fitzhenry.ca

Acknowledgements

The author is indebted to the kindness of the following for their generous help and assistance in furnishing data for this work:

Mrs. Violet May for placing at my disposal documents, records, photographs and clippings of the late Captain Wilfred Reid May; Mr. C. M. G. Farrell for furnishing invaluable information and data; Mr. H. A. "Doc" Oaks and Mr. John Reid for photographs; Mr. S. A. Tomlinson for his technical assistance and details concerning the early days of bush-flying in both Eastern and Western Canada and the work of the "Black-Gang"; Mr. J. A. Wilson of Air Services, Department of Transport; Mr. A. Kirby, Public Relations Officer, Post Office Department, Calgary, for verifying information concerning the first Arctic Air Mail; and the Wartime Information Board for information concerning the Alaska Highway and the Northwest Staging Route.

Dedicated to

My wife, Jean, herself a Northern pioneer, whose help throughout the years has been invaluable.

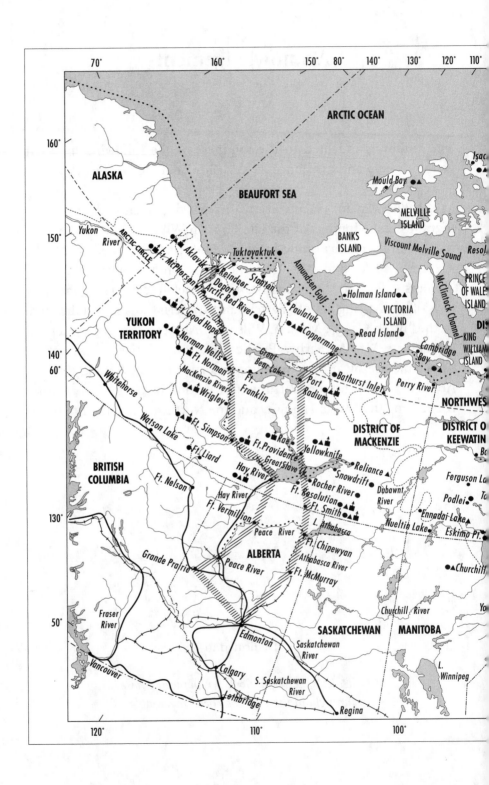

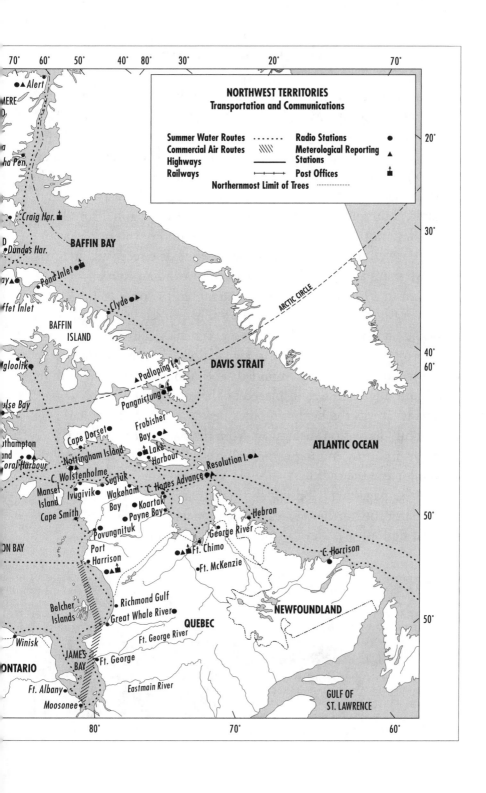

70° 60° 50° 40° 80° 30° 20° 70°

NORTHWEST TERRITORIES
Transportation and Communications

Summer Water Routes ······
Commercial Air Routes \\\\\
Highways ——————
Railways +————+

Radio Stations ●
Meterological Reporting ▲
Stations
Post Offices ▲

Northernmost Limit of Trees ----------

20°
30°

●▲ Alert
MERE
D
a
ha Pen.

● Craig Har. ▲
Dunda's Har.
BAFFIN BAY
ay▲●
●Pond Inlet ▲●
ffet Inlet
Clyde ●▲

ARCTIC CIRCLE

BAFFIN
ISLAND

gloolik ●

Ise Bay

DAVIS STRAIT

40°
60°

▲Padloping I.
Pangnirtung ■

Cape Dorset●
Frobisher
Bay ● ●
▲ Lake
Harbour
Nottingham Island

ATLANTIC OCEAN

uthampton
and
oral Harbour ●
C. Wolstenholme ●
Suglük ●
Resolution I.●▲
Mansel
Island
Ivugivik●
Wakeham
Bay
C. Hopes Advance ●
Koartak ●
Payne Bay ●
Hebron ●

50°

Cape Smith
Povungnituk ●
George River ●
ON BAY
Port
Harrison ●
●▲▲ Ft. Chimo
●▲ ▲
Ft. McKenzie ●
C. Harrison ●

Belcher
Islands
● Richmond Gulf
Great Whale River●
NEWFOUNDLAND

50°

QUEBEC
Ft. George River
Winisk

JAMES
BAY
●Ft. George
ONTARIO

Eastmain River

GULF OF
ST. LAWRENCE

Ft. Albany●
Moosonee●

80° 70° 60°

About the Author

Philip H. Godsell, F.R.G.S., F.R.E.S., former inspecting officer for the Hudson's Bay Company, and Member of the exclusive Explorers Club of New York, knew the Far North intimately. Nobody was in a better position than Mr. Godsell to appreciate the revolutionary impact made on the North by the aeroplane and the pioneer bush-pilots. His trails carried him by dog-team, canoe, York boat and pack-train a hundred thousand miles through the wilderness from Labrador to Alaska, and north to the Arctic Islands. Life in the "Interior" was one of utter isolation. In those days the lonely exiles received, at times, only two mails a year by dog-team, canoe, or Indian *courier*.

When, in 1921, the first Junker attempted to conquer the North, only to crash at Fort Simpson, it was Philip Godsell who supplied the man and materials to make the now famed "sleigh-board, moose-glue" prop that carried it back to civilization. Then, a few short years later, the North became air-minded. The colourful *voyageur* with his canoe and dog-team was displaced by the bush pilot with his winged aeroplane. It was the beginning of a new era! Where there had been naught but desolation there arose from the barren rocks thriving settlements and busy mining camps, all linked with the Outside by the bush pilot and the radio.

In these pages Mr. Godsell tells in dramatic prose the story of the conquest of the northern skies by the pioneer bush pilots, who, literally and figuratively, "flew by the seat of their pants."

Philip Godsell beside canoe on bank of Liard River, Northwest Territories. *Glenbow Archives NA-2563-8*

Foreword

Air transport in Canada has progressed at such an astonishing pace during the past two decades that the fabulous era of the pioneer bush pilot already seems to belong to another age. Today, as modern airliners drone across the vast hinterlands extending from the end of steel to the Arctic Ocean, much of the early adventure has disappeared from northern skies. The dramatic testing of human ingenuity and skill against the fierce elements of the northland has been succeeded by the less eventful, more prosaic conquest of these same elements by precision instrument flying, by modern airline equipment and technique.

In our preoccupation with this new phase, we are in danger of forgetting the heritage of the pioneer period. It is indeed fortunate that a factual and interesting record of Canadian bush pilot exploits has now become available. Written by an experienced author, with the unique advantage of first-hand knowledge and experience, this book is a most important contribution to our air history. It is also a fascinating narrative.

G. W. G. McConachie.
President, Canadian Pacific Airlines
1955

Contents

"For I dipt into the future, far as human eye could see,
Saw the Vision of the world, and all the wonder that would be.
Saw the heavens fill with commerce, argosies of magic sails,
Pilots of the purple twilight, dropping down with costly bales;
Heard the heavens fill with shouting, and there rain'd a ghastly dew
From the nations' airy navies grappling in the central blue."

Tennyson, *Locksley Hall.*

THE
BECKONING
NORTH

When Gavrilo Princip, the Serb student, sent a bullet crashing into Archduke Francis Ferdinand, the heir to the Austrian Empire, in Sarajevo, Bosnia, that peaceful summer day of June 28, 1914, he not only "fired the shot heard round the world" but loosed the fingers of Fate which were to set the feet of men upon strange paths, and tear asunder forever the barriers of distance that had been the bulwark of the peace the universe had enjoyed. As with all world-shattering events, few realized to the full the impact this "European incident" was to have upon the lives of all and sundry—even people unborn. On August 4, 1914, the law of self-preservation, linked with desperation and necessity, set in motion forces that were to carry science and invention to new and undreamed of heights and send mankind, literally and figuratively, flying into strange new worlds.

For nearly half a century the Western world had lived under the inertia of tranquillity and peace, enjoying the diffused plenty of cheapness and freedom no living being was ever to see again. Though newspapers spoke of a world catastrophe their message conveyed little, or nothing, to those for whom the world had always seemed safe and secure. In homes all across the land there was much talk and excited conjecture but it was the talk and conjecture of spectators who had no true sense or realization of the part they were to play in the catastrophic upheaval which was to involve and engulf them all. The world was about to be set on fire, yet the conflagration was a nebulous thing—a distant miasma which couldn't possibly affect the little individual worlds of the populace at large. But, as event piled upon event, and the German Army prepared to spread its evil despite all treaties and decencies, the picture began to assume a different colour. Soon the youth of the land, caught up in the fever and excitement of the moment, were rushing to the recruiting stations to sign up for the "Big Adventure," and Wilfred Reid May of Carberry, Manitoba, was no exception, though he little realized when he took the King's Shilling that his part in this adventure was ultimately to place his name, along with those of other fellow Canadians and trail-blazers of the war, high on the roster of North American aviation.

Known as "Wop" as far back as his school-days, nobody could accuse him of having Latin blood in his veins. A tall, pronounced blond, slim and active as a panther, he was as demonstrative as the Sphinx and about as communicative as the proverbial oyster. Actually, the nickname, which clung to him throughout his life, was acquired when the little daughter of Judge Swanson of Kamloops, lisped the name Wilfred into something that resembled "Wop."

The moving fingers of Fate dealt the first cards in "Wop's" ultimate destiny and that of Northern bush flying when, in 1902, the family decided to move west to Edmonton, Northwest Territories, which, three years later, was to become the Province of Alberta. The future capital of the Northwest was just emerging from its chrysalis and throwing off the primitive rule of the Fur Lords. The end of the ox-cart era was still not far behind. In fact, a cavalcade of squeaking Red River carts, drawn by oxen, still hauled the Hudson's Bay Company's freight and fur-packs across Smith Portage to the northward, while a regular brigade of horse-drawn Bain wagons, with their swarthy half-breed drivers, was in constant motion over the Athabasca Trail, hauling supplies for the northern trading posts from Edmonton to Athabasca Landing and returning with the baled wealth of the Silent Places.

On the banks of the swift-flowing Saskatchewan, where the old Hudson's Bay Company's post—Fort Edmonton—still reared its squat trading stores and grey stockades, bronzed Crees continued to barter their peltries with the factors, while, only a few years before, a hunting party had sought sanctuary within its palisades when predatory Blackfeet had pursued them to the very gates. A straggling street, fronted with ugly, square-faced stores, harness shops, livery stables and the inevitable Chinese cafés—all smelling of newly-sawn lumber—lined the heights above, rubbing shoulders with the Queen's Hotel and its more aristocratic competitor, the Alberta Hotel, across the way. Aloof and dignified stood the whitewashed buildings which housed the red-coated members of "N" Division of the Royal North West Mounted Police[1] under the command of the veteran Inspector Wroughton.

1. Founded in 1873, the Force was known as the North West Mounted Police until 1902 when the name became Royal North West Mounted Police. Later, in 1920, the name was changed once more to—Royal Canadian Mounted Police.—P.H.G.

Edmonton was still a frontier town. The steel tentacles of the Canadian Pacific Railway had reached a halt at Strathcona, on the south side, though the Canadian Northern and Grand Trunk were uncoiling twin ribbons of steel slowly across the prairies to the eastward.

High hopes stalked the muddy streets of this city of contrasts where the ox-cart was to dodge the automobile, French heels sink in moccasin tracks, and the high silk hat salute the stiff-brimmed Stetson. It was, as it still is, the gateway to that vast, picturesque and, then, untamed two million square miles of rugged mountains, pathless forests, rushing rivers and tranquil lakes enjoying the comprehensive title "The North." From its muddy streets, log buildings and frame shacks fur traders, half-breed freighters, grizzled trappers, priests and black-cowled nuns from the seminaries of Montreal and Quebec trekked north by canoe, pack-train and stern-wheeler to the rolling prairies of the Peace, the forested wilds of the Athabasca, and the far-distant Mackenzie region wherein the Hudson's Bay Company, undisturbed by the surrender of their Royal Charter thirty-odd years before, still held feudal sway under the despotic regime of Chief Factor William Thomas Livock who ruled with an iron hand encased in velvet from his palisaded stronghold on the river-bank.

A slim, reserved and, at times, somewhat moody youngster, the North was soon putting its ineradicable mark upon "Wop" May as, annually, the giants of the *Pays d'en Haut* and the voyageurs of the Three Rivers converged on the fast-growing frontier town. There was Angus Brabant, eagle-eyed potentate of the Mackenzie; Colin Fraser, free trader from Fort Chipewyan on the shores of beautiful, island-dotted Athabasca Lake, who had defied the might of the "Gentlemen Adventurers" to trade furs on his own from coppery Slavies and Chipewyans, a man whose great-grandfather had been piper to Governor Simpson, the Little Emperor of Rupert's Land, as he travelled from the Atlantic to the Pacific in his gaily-painted *canot-de-maitre*. There was Captain Haight, "Admiral" of the Hudson's Bay scow transport, with his brass-buttoned uniform, foghorn voice, and colourful vocabulary; "Peace River Jim" Cornwall, who had participated in the march of Coxey's Army on Washington then headed west to establish the firm of Bredin and Cornwall and compete with the Hudson's Bay Company for the Indian trade of the Peace River country, and that roguish Highland chieftain, Campbell Young, of Hislop and Nagle, whose picketed fur forts stood cheek by jowl with those of the Company the length of the far-off Mackenzie. There was Jack Hornby, too, the bearded Hermit of the Barrens who had once trained for the British Diplomatic Service and who was destined to die of starvation with his two young companions in the heart of the Barrens he loved—and others hated. And, no one could forget granite-featured Sergeant Anderson of the Royal North West Mounted Police. Around hotel lobbies the story was told of how this giant Icelander with the pock-pitted face and ice-blue eyes once dogged a criminal for months only to find him buried in the fastnesses of the, then, almost inaccessible Pouce Coupe country. To prove to Headquarters that he had caught up with his quarry, "Andy" calmly dug up the body, cut off the head and brought the grisly object back in a gunny-sack to a very unappreciative Officer Commanding. When he boarded the train at the end-of-steel there was something about the sinister bundle that aroused the coloured porter's curiosity. As the Sergeant snored blissfully he hooked the gunny-sack from beneath the bunk and lifted it. The repulsive head rolled down the aisle, evoking screams that echoed throughout the train. Old-timers still insist that porter is running yet!

As these husky Northerners swept into town, in company with their Indian or half-breed retainers, by dog-drawn *carriole* or stage, the columns of the local press recorded stories of hair-raising adventure on trail and trap-line. Each summer, too, *The Journal* and *The Bulletin* displayed pictures depicting the annual treaty party en route to the Far North to carry King Edward's treaty money to nomad Slavey, Yellow-Knife and Dog-Rib Indians, while Jim Cornwall made the welkin ring with his praises of the "New North," and his attempt to slash a frontier railroad from Edmonton to Fort McMurray to open up the Athabasca, the Slave and the Mackenzie rivers.

To any impressionable lad with the spirit of adventure in his soul these things could scarcely help but prove an inspiration and the youthful May, along with others like him, proved no exception to the rule. By the time he was sixteen, settlers from as far south as Iowa and Texas were battling the muskegs along the widely-advertised and much misrepresented Edson Trail to carve out a new empire in the North. Every day saw a further incursion, and exodus, of this seemingly endless covered-wagon caravan as the last mass movement of whites into the unoccupied lands of the Northwest continued.

While the Mounted Police were kept busy in their eternal search for illicit booze the unorganized caravan continued to trickle in and out of town, some heading for the Edson Trail while wiser ones branched off along the Athabasca Trail to Lesser Slave Lake and the rolling highlands beyond Peace River Crossing. Every day one heard new tales of hope or hardship, or tragedy and humour, while the evanescent hope of the new pioneer settlers was reflected in the slogans scrawled on their wagon-covers or the rickety sides of their cabooses: "Grande Prairie or Bust!" "Peace River or Bust!" "Grand Falls to Grande Prairie!"

Enthralled by this passing pageant of pioneering humanity, "Wop" never missed an opportunity to know what was going on. Eagerly he talked to nasal-toned Easterners and soft-spoken Yankees, and read with avidity McKitterick's stories—hot from Dunvegan, The Waterhole, Peace River and Grande Prairie—of this stampede into the new "Promised Land."

That tragedy stalked these Northern trails was forcibly brought home to him when word reached a shocked Edmonton of the death by starvation of Inspector Francis J. Fitzgerald of the Royal North West Mounted Police, and the lost Dawson Patrol, comprising Constables Carter, Kinney and Taylor, in the snow-filled passes of the Arctic Rockies east of Fort McPherson—an area with which "Wop," himself, was to become only too familiar in the years ahead.

That same summer, along the streets of Edmonton, "Wop" and other future bush fliers gazed with fascinated eyes as the stuffed wood-buffalo, slain by the ill-fated explorers, Radford and Street, was paraded along First Street. As though to top off the day's excitement, the evening *Bulletin* carried the story, in banner headlines, of

Vihljalmur Stefansson's new biological discovery amongst the Arctic snows to the northward—of the so-called "blue-eyed, blonde" Eskimos.

"Some day," "Wop" told his brother, Court, after hearing from the lips of bronzed Northerners how Radford and Street had fallen victims to the copper snow-knives of these same Eskimos on the icy shore of Bathurst Inlet, "I'm going into that country and you'll hear of *me* down there!"

Court grinned with good-natured tolerance, little realizing how truly prophetic these words were going to prove.

At Victoria High School in Edmonton, May formed a firm friendship with Roy Brown of Carleton Place, Ontario. A slim, dark-haired chap with square jaw and shrewd grey eyes, Roy exuded an expansive friendliness. Both shared a love of sports—sailing, lacrosse and the track—and Roy had gained the reputation of being one of the outstanding baseball and hockey players in the city. Added to all this, they also shared a common interest in the then undeveloped science of aviation and would spend hours together discussing the significance of the Wright brothers' first flight in a heavier-than-air machine. How, on December 17, 1903, Orville had succeeded in covering 120-feet at a height of 50-feet in twelve seconds in a twenty-one-mile-an-hour wind from a base near the village of Kitty Hawk, North Carolina, on historic Roanoke Island where Raleigh's Lost Colony predated the settlements of Plymouth and Jamestown, while, that same day, Wilbur soared 852-feet in fifty seconds. The fact that Louis Bleriot had been successful in flying the English Channel from Calais to Dover in only thirty-seven minutes six years later appealed to each of them as an assurance that, despite the much-advertised and abortive attempt at a flight put on at the Edmonton Exhibition grounds not long afterwards, the aeroplane had come into its own.

Yet, nobody in Edmonton, least of all young Brown and May, could have foreseen the time when this frontier city, only just emerging from the ox-cart and dog-team era, was to become the cradle of aerial pioneering and development for the vast hinterland lying to the northward. Neither could they, in their wildest dreams, have foreseen that in this same forested wilderness the old-time *voyageur* with his canoe and dog-team was to yield pride of place to the bush-pilot with his winged aeroplane, or that the small but rapidly-growing city on the banks of the Saskatchewan was to give birth to a new but equally indomitable type of pioneer—his "canoe" an aeroplane and his "paddle" a propellor—the khaki-clad bush-pilot who was to blaze new sky-trails from the end-of-steel to the Polar Sea. For the days when Edmonton, with its two splendidly-equipped modern airports, was to proudly proclaim itself "the cross-roads of the world," and send Russian-bound, lend-lease bombers winging their way over the Northwest Staging Route for delivery to Soviet girl-pilots at Fairbanks, Alaska, to be used in blasting Hitler's Nazi hordes from Russian soil, still lay deep in the future. Yet the dark clouds which were already threatening in distant Europe were to nurture many of these embryonic bush-fliers who would be moulded to their future destiny in the fiery crucible of war.

2

MAKING
OF A PILOT

The West, busy with the opening up of new frontiers to the northward, was totally unprepared for the events that were to jolt it to its very core on that fateful day, August 4, 1914, when the declaration of war with Germany struck like a thunderbolt from the blue. By stuttering telegraph key word sped over the wires to Lesser Slave Lake, to Peace River Crossing and to the much-advertised but diminutive Dunvegan. From Grande Prairie, Spirit River and The Waterhole the "moccasin telegraph" soon carried the word into the remotest parts.

Billy Griesbach, son of the first man to enlist in the North West Mounted Police—and a former trooper of "C" Squadron of the Strathcona Horse who had seen his own share of battle and hardship in South Africa during the Boer War—now proceeded to organize the famed 49th Battalion, or Edmonton Regiment. Soon it gathered into its ranks not only raw recruits from the Silent Places but many original members of the North West Mounted Police who had also served throughout the South African campaign.

Not until 1916 was "Wop" May able to join, with his friend, Ray Ross, the 202nd, or so-called "Sportsman's Battalion," under the command of Colonel J. J. Bowlen, the present Lieutenant-Governor of Alberta.

Already the Uhlans, the eyes and ears of the German Army, had been superseded by the aeroplane, and dog-fights in the skies above contending armies had become an accepted part of the battle picture.

Thumbing through a copy of *The Illustrated London News* a few weeks before joining up, "Wop's" eyes lighted at the picture of Allied planes strafing a column of retreating German Infantry frantically attempting to escape the merciless leaden hail that poured down upon them. Another artist's drawing depicted a German Staff car undergoing a similar aerial bombardment. "That," "Wop" chuckled as he tossed the periodical to Ray, "is the way to fight. When you're up in the air like that you've got them where you want them. Why, you're moving so fast they haven't a chance to pick you off. To *hell* with slogging through Flanders mud on foot. It's me for the Flying Corps!"

Finding that only the Infantry lay open to them they made a virtue of necessity and permitted their spirit of patriotism and adventure to land them in the ranks of the 202nd Battalion, hoping to transfer to the Royal Flying Corps later in England. After a short but intensive period of training they were on their way to France.

A year and a half later "Wop" had his wish fulfilled. From a Sergeant in the Machine Gun section of the 202nd he found himself transferred to England for a course of training in the now vastly expanding Royal Flying Corps. "Wop" has left a brief but illuminating record of what that training was like:

In those days I trained on a Caudron aeroplane fighter machine with rotary engine. It was a tractor 'plane. Instead of the regular ailerons the wings were made of bamboo, and they certainly warped and bent, so it doesn't require much imagination to visualize the kind of machines they were. You didn't learn to fly in the usual way. They taught you to fly up the field, take off in the field—and land in the field again. The first trip I made I was feeling pretty cocky. I was in the air at last! I took it into my head that I'd like to show them a little fancy flying. I performed the figure eight in the ether, strictly contrary to the accepted letter of instructions, and succeeded in landing in an adjoining field right side up—much to the wrathful astonishment of my Instructor, who figured we should both have been killed.

My first real trip was even more eventful and, once again, a beneficent Providence must have been hovering over me. I was taken in a Bristol Fighter to Northolt Airport along with an observer when, from out of the blue, an R. E. 8 landed squarely on top of us. Yet, by some miracle, not one of us got scratched.

Somehow, by the divine intervention of Providence, I succeeded in getting through my training—and, believe me, it was rough—without breaking any bones, or creating any casualties, much to the surprise of my instructors and the Mess—who foretold for me a quick and early demise—and was posted to a Scout.

My first solo, in a Camel, was not devoid of startling incidents. We were to pick up a single-seater aircraft at Northolt Airport. Whilst heading there to take over, I saw my prospective machine

Lieutenant Wilfred Reid "Wop" May, of Edmonton, Alberta, 1917.
Glenbow Archives NA-1258-2

come down on my Instructor in a mass of tangled wreckage. Next moment there was a thundering detonation, a blinding sheet of flame and wreckage being spewed in all directions to the cacophony of screaming sirens as crash cars, ambulances and fire-trucks hurtled to the spot.

As I watched the rescue crews haul the charred and mutilated remains of my former Instructor from the twisted wreckage I lost all heart for any more flying that day. But, the training was tough and the first thing I knew I was in the air, solo. Somehow I managed to fly ten thousand faltering feet without even turning—my mind still tortured by the tragedy I'd witnessed. Next day I was ordered to Scotland for my gunnery course. I got there that night. The following afternoon I was hustled back to London. My "gunnery course" was over!

Promptly I was shipped across to France. Times were grim, and even raw pilots were needed to replace the terrific loss being sustained in the Flying Corps as the Fifth Army was battered relentlessly westward. I found myself posted to a pilot's pool at St. Omar, just west of the Belgian border, where we were to remain until sent as replacements for those shot out of the sky. I soon found myself rubbing shoulders with other lads from the Land of the Maple Leaf: that wiry atom of human dynamite, "Con" Farrell from Minnedosa; the ubiquitous Walter Gilbert from Cardinal, with his sardonic sense of humour; stolid Lieutenant George Gorman, always wrapped in sombre aloofness, and a dozen others I was to meet again years later winging their crates through the frigid skies of Canada's Northwest Territories in that unending yen for adventure that was sparked on these blood-stained battlefields.

Around the Mess I ran into another air-minded chap I'd met in the old 49th. As we lifted our elbows at the bar he suggested I take a flier with him over the enemy lines next morning. Somehow I wasn't able to make it. Poor devil, his ship was shot out of the air in a blaze of pyrotechnics, and what reached the ground you couldn't have put in a match-box. Finally, I was posted to the 9th Naval Squadron at Bertangles. I was in the Royal Naval Air Service at last!

Believe me, there's quite a difference between the training squadrons over in Blighty and the highly-disciplined and orderly Royal Naval Air Service. Having still retained a little of the old, independent Western spirit, and not yet fully appreciative of the difference, I accepted the invitation of a congenial buddy to accompany him on an unscheduled motor trip of a hundred and fifty-odd miles to some spot that still remains vague in my mind. We had the time of our lives. Days and nights merged into one grand fling. The wine was like nectar—the girls positively enchanting. I was stepping on golden clouds! When I finally got back to my squadron, somewhat bedraggled both in mind and appearance, and unable to determine how I was going to explain this time-lapse, Major Butler, the stern and dignified British Officer Commanding, proved to be regretfully lacking in the saving grace of humour.

Granite-faced, and oozing discipline from every pore, he laid down the law in no uncertain terms. He was through with me, he snapped in clipped, incisive tones. He was having no part of me at all. He was returning me, forthwith—and *without* his blessing—to the pilots' pool and . . . be *damned* to me!

I slunk out of his vitriolic presence with my tail between my legs to report to the Adjutant and take my medicine. Feeling mighty sorry for myself, I glanced around and found myself staring into the familiar, square-jawed face of Roy Brown, my old friend of Victoria High School days in Edmonton. Captain Brown now, he was Flight Leader in the 209th Squadron near Bertangles. But, this wasn't the Roy Brown I'd known in Edmonton. This man was lean and haggard, his face criss-crossed with lines of fatigue from the tension of too many nerve-wracking, whirling aerial combats. He looked as though he'd just come out of hospital except for that undiminished glint in his grey eyes.

"For God's sake—'Wop'!" He emitted an astonished roar and pounded me on the back. "Well, I'll be *damned!*"

He laughed when I finished relating my madcap escapade. "I'll try and fix things up. I'll speak to your O.C., and tell him I'll be responsible for you and take you into my flight in exchange for one of my own men." He flashed his big, friendly smile. "I'm sure things will come out all right."

The ensuing minutes seemed like hours as I gazed disconsolately through the window of the Orderly Room at the huge Bossaneau hangars and waited whilst Roy remained closeted with Major Butler. Finally he emerged, and I knew by the grin on his face everything was O.K.

Brown's squadron, under the command of Major C. H. Butler, D.S.C., was located at Bertangles, cooperating with the British Fifth Army on the Amiens front. Back at the base there, "Wop" learned that Roy, after leaving Edmonton, had gone to Wright's Flying School at Dayton, Ohio, to study aviation at his own expense. With this United States training he had gained a commission as a Flight Sub-Lieutenant in the British Royal Navy in September, 1915, and had sailed in December from New York for England. While undergoing combat training at Chingford he had crashed, fractured a spinal vertebra, and been confined to hospital till 1917.

Until April 1, 1918, Brown had flown with the Royal Navy Air Squadron No. 9, assigned to duty in France, his unit patrolling the Belgian coast, and escorting bombing raids far behind the German lines. Officially, he was credited with having knocked down twelve enemy planes, though his buddies insisted that this figure did not begin to approach the actual number of German machines he had blasted from the skies. Despite the modesty of his reports, he had been awarded the Distinguished Flying Cross in recognition of his work.

Fourteen months of the strain and uncertainty of constant aerial combat and hair-raising escapes combined with longer days and nights in the shell-torn war zone had placed their mark on Roy. Shattered nerves and a refractory stomach, "Wop" learned, had necessitated his living for the past four weeks on a daily diet of brandy and milk.

May, Roy discovered, was one of a group of airmen whose advanced training in England had been abruptly terminated due to the fact that pilots were so desperately needed in France to replace the many lost in action above the Somme.

"Roy gave me as much training as he could behind the lines, which wasn't much," May wrote in April, 1918. "He'd lead us over the lines in his cherry-nosed Sopwith Camel to get shot-up by anti-aircraft fire. It wasn't very accurate in those days, and rarely did the burst come close enough to give us much concern."

Around the Mess at Bertangles there was one dominant topic of conversation. The astounding exploits and invulnerability of the daring and resourceful Baron Manfred von Richthofen, the so-called Red Knight of the Air, and his flying circus of deadly Albatross Scouts and Fokkers D VII's, who was raising more than his fair share of blazing hell, tearing ragged holes in the pilots' pool and all but dominating the air in whatever section he was flying his scarlet-painted triplane.

Born in Breslau on May 2, 1892, the son of an officer in the dreaded Uhlan Regiment who had spent his lifetime fighting—adding, between times, his own share of trophies of the hunt to the already considerable number decorating the walls of his ancestral home in Schweidnitz, German Silesia—Richthofen was imbued from childhood with the primitive urge to hunt and kill. By the summer of 1918 he had shot down eighty enemy planes in matching his life against that of his adversaries. It was said, however, that he fought not with hate but for the pure love of aerial combat. It had become his one absorbing joy and passion. Wounded, and decorated, he had become a national hero and the youth of the German nation made him their idol. He had the courage to kill, and be killed.

Despite the many to fall victim to his flying circus, the Flying Corps recognized something sporting in the unflinching code of the handsome, bold-eyed War Ace for, into the grisly story of blood and carnage, there came a refreshing gleam of the chivalry of old when the pick of Allied and German youth carried the war into the skies. In this Knighthood of the Heavens Richthofen had been awarded a place of the highest merit by those who fought both with and against him. In other words, he won, and held, the admiration that brave foes hold in their breasts for each other.

Richthofen's Circus had its headquarters just east of the little village of Cappy. On the morning of April 21 he rose with a feeling of elation, the congratulations of his pilots still ringing in his ears from his eightieth victory of the day before. Added to this exultation was the happy prospect of going home on leave two days hence, and big game hunting in the Black Forest. He and Lieutenant Wolff had already planned to spend their leave together, flying their machines back to Friedberg if the weather permitted. As an alternative they agreed to use the railroad—and had already purchased their tickets.

As Richthofen stepped out of his quarters, radiating pride, robust health and self-confidence, he was serenaded by a regimental band which had been sent over to the airdrome by a nearby Division Commander who desired, in this way, to tender his personal congratulations to the invincible Ace. But, somehow, the music did not appeal to him. In company with Wolff, he hurried over to the hangar where mechanics were tuning up his plane. One of the men stepped forward with a postcard addressed to his son back in Germany and asked the Baron to autograph it. "So! You think I won't return!" He smiled grimly as he inscribed his signature.

At exactly 10:30 British time, Staffell II, comprising three groups of five planes each, soared into the air. The Red Knight led the first group while Lieutenants Karjus and Wolff headed the others. At the same time Staffell V, also under Richthofen's command, took to the air and headed west towards the Front.

Twenty-odd miles away, separated by the thousands of mud-begrimed human moles burrowing in fox-holes and trenches who comprised the fighting units of two mighty military forces engaged in mortal combat, Roy Brown rolled from his bunk with his usual queasy stomach and shattered nerves, tossed down his breakfast of brandy and milk and headed for the hangars.

Camel after Camel was rolled out. Ground crews swarmed over them and Clerget engines broke into life, coughing and barking unevenly. Composed of three flights of five planes each, Roy's squadron took to the air at about the same time as Richthofen's. When Brown noticed that Major Butler and his five planes had been lost sight of he promptly assumed command and signalled the rest of the flight to take position behind him.

Flying in wide arcs, the squadron gained an altitude of 15,000-feet and, with a characteristic aggressiveness, proceeded to probe into the enemy air-zone. The throaty bass roar of ten engines flooded the ether to the exclusion of all other sound. Wings glistening in the April sunshine, rising and falling gently like small boats on soft sea swells, the planes prowled the sky, each pilot alone with his thoughts as he scanned the blue for signs of enemy planes.

May, sitting stiffly in his bucket seat, was flying in the last position on the left leg of Brown's flight. A thin, gossamer haze lessened the visibility but, in the distance, he could barely see the front sectors, jagged and overcast with smoke-needled pin-pricks of orange gunfire. An hour droned by, a dull, boring hour that rasped taut nerves keyed for action. Then came the first break in the monotonous patrol—a prelude to the bitter dog-fight to come.

A great gust of black smoke unfolded like a suddenly-opened umbrella as one of his squadron mates slipped up on an Albatross D-5 and sent it reeling down in flames with his first burst. Other Camels trailed after the aggressive pilot, giving him tail-protection, and then more Camels, their pilots sensing action at last, broke formation and raced after the trio.

Far below, Brown spotted a couple of hard-pressed, antiquated R 8 observation planes desperately attempting to shake off four hungry enemy Fokkers. Old, slow, creaking two-seaters, they were no match for the attacking "tripes." Brown waggled his wings, the signal for attack, thrust forward the control stick and slammed downward in a long, bowling dive towards the uneven engagement. "Wop" recalled what happened in vivid words:

> With the limited experience I had I didn't see what Brown was going down on when he wobbled his wings to attack. Just before we took off, Roy had given me instructions since this was to be

my initiation in actual combat. I was to stay up on top when he went down to attack enemy aircraft and just watch and see how things went. "If we tangle with the Jerries," he told me, "stay clear. If you get an opportunity to pick off one, remember—*dive* on him. Give him a burst then—*streak like hell for home.* If you down an e.a., swell! If you *don't*—and run for home—nobody's going to hold it against you. *Remember*—don't let yourself get dragged into any dog-fight!"

As instructed, I stayed up, circling, but didn't see an enemy aircraft till one of them materialized right beneath me. I dived to the attack, missed—and followed him down. In the midst of a droning swarm of enemy planes that seemed to hurtle up from every direction, I continued my attack—let go still another hail of gunfire and saw my quarry mushroom into an ebony cloud of trailing smoke and plummet like a fiery meteor towards the earth.

Enemy "tripes" were coming at me from all sides now. The sky was alive with combat planes. Wings were all about me, the staccato roar of machine-gun fire rising above the vicious drone of the motors. Some, I missed by inches. Overwhelmed by the fury of the attacking squadrons, I went into a vertical turn, held my guns open and sought to spray as many as I could. The fight was at such incredibly close quarters that dozens of enemy planes dipped and swooped about me. Next moment my guns jammed—first one and then the other—leaving me defenceless. Somehow, I spun out of the fierce dog-fight and headed west for home.

After I regained my breath and levelled off I gazed around me but not a soul was on my tail. I patted myself on the back at my miraculous escape, climbed to ten-thousand-feet and proceeded to work my way west. But my feeling of elation wasn't destined to last long. The first thing I knew I received a burst of gunfire from the rear. Unable to fight back, all I could do was to try and dodge my pursuer. I noticed it was a flaming red triplane—but if I'd realized it was Richthofen, the dreaded Red Knight of the Air, I'd have probably passed out on the spot!

I kept dodging, spinning, looping—doing every trick I knew—until I ran out of sky and was forced to hedge-hop over the ground. Richthofen was giving me burst after burst from his twin Spandau machine-guns. The only thing that saved me was my awful flying! I didn't know what I was doing myself, and I'm certain Richthofen couldn't figure out what I was going to do next. Ground-fire sprayed us as we passed over, first, the German, then the British lines.

After almost slicing off the tops of some of the hedges, I found myself skimming the surface of the Somme, with Richthofen still hanging onto my tail, and proceeded to round a curve in the river near Corbie. But Richthofen beat me to it and swooped down on me from over the hill. I knew I was a sitting duck. I must have died a dozen deaths. Every second I expected the stream of Spandau bullets to tear a hole right through me. I was too low down between the banks to make a turn away from him. He simply had me, *cold!* I was in such a state of mind that I had to restrain myself from pushing the stick forward and diving into the water. In my mind's eye I could see the leather-helmeted head of my enemy, his goggled-eyes lining his Spandau for the kill.

Another plane flitted past the tail of my eye, followed by a burst of gunfire and—a sudden silence! As I threw a fearful glance over my shoulder I saw Richthofen do a half-spin and hit the ground. A second glance showed me that the second plane was one of our own.

Not until I headed towards the airport with my rescuer did I realize that I owed my life to my old school-chum, Roy Brown. Two enemy aircraft, he told me later, were on his tail when he happened to see Richthofen's red triplane dive upon me like a hawk. Hurtling in pursuit, he'd found the Red Knight so engrossed in knocking me down that he'd succeeded in getting into firing position and giving him one short burst. The bullet entered the Baron's back, near the shoulder, and penetrated his heart—killing him instantly.

That the Baron didn't hit me with any of his fire can be attributed, without doubt, to my unrehearsed aerobatics and extraordinarily bad flying—all of which, unquestionably, saved my life. The only bullet holes in my machine were through the wings and fuselage. When Brown landed beside me at Bertangles there were fifty bullet holes in his plane—and only half the cylinders working.

I was told, afterwards, that Richthofen didn't fly with his Circus but preferred to stay aloft in the sun, where he couldn't be seen, waiting for cripples to limp out of a dog-fight then he'd swoop down on them and shatter them to pieces, with little danger to himself. Perhaps this explains why I was allowed to stagger out of the dog-fight, unmolested—to be left to Richthofen's "tender mercy"!

Hardly had the news of Roy Brown's victory over Germany's Air Ace reached the trenches than a bitter controversy split the ranks. An Australian air-gunner claimed that the red "tripe" had been shot out of the air, as it glided over the Australian lines, by Corporal Wilson of the 64th Artillery Battery. To settle the question, a post-mortem was held by Army and Air medical officers who agreed that Richthofen had died from a single bullet which, after entering his back on the right had traversed his heart and emerged through his left breast. Having probed the wound, they went on record to the effect that "the situation and exit of wounds are such that they could not have been caused by ground fire." Yet, despite this finding, the controversy has continued on down the years, with little to bolster the Australian claim.

While doubt continued to exist on the Allied side as to who had actually brought the Red Knight of the Air down, the entire German Air Force was stunned. For the first time in his long and successful career the Baron had failed to return! Was he killed—or captured?

Lieutenant Wolff, who regarded himself as the German air-leader's appointed protector, scoffed at the idea that any British pilot could have shot down his friend from the rear. German pilots flew over the lines, desperately searching out the red triplane—which their observers reported as having landed near Corbie. Ground officers scoured the sky with powerful range-finders in the vain hope of sighting the missing Fokker. Ugly rumours swept the German lines. Richthofen, it was charged, had been shot in cold blood after making a normal landing behind the British lines. Threats of reprisal filled the air.

The last hope that the Baron had survived was shattered on the night of April 21 when his death was announced through official British channels. The following day, as Richthofen's body lay in state in a British tent-hangar at Bertangles, all British airmen who could be present paid a silent tribute to their fallen foe.

Of the scarlet Fokker with the twin Spandau machine-guns, which had sent so many of the boys to a merciless death, little remained when souvenir-hunters got through with it. Despite his ultimate fate, an aura of good luck seemed to surround the equipment of the man whose tremendous and lasting success in the air had blazoned his name throughout the world, and many of the boys indulged in subconscious superstition by ripping off bits of fabric to carry with them on their hazardous flights aloft.

But Roy Brown, like "Wop," kept aloof from the death-tent, the Spandaus and the wreckage. While comrades invaded his quarters to congratulate him on his victory, Roy displayed an aversion to discussing the subject. As the body of the Red Knight lay in state Brown was in the air again, engaging the embittered units of Staffell II, now really out for blood to avenge their fallen leader.

Brown had no recollection of returning from that patrol, and recalled little that happened during the ensuing weeks. Landing his Camel safely back behind the lines, he collapsed in the pilot's seat and was rushed to hospital at Amiens, suffering from a serious stomach and intestinal ailment aggravated by intense nervous and physical strain. Placed on the critical list, he remained for three weeks in a semi-delirious state. Within six weeks, however, he resumed duty as Combat Instructor in England, where the Prince of Wales pinned an additional Bar on his Distinguished Flying Cross.

Providence, which had looked after young May so effectively, did not desert him, and many of the veterans of the First Great War still recall how, misled by the blond youngster's disarming manner, they had been foolhardy enough to let him take them up for a flip. When they staggered from the plane, green around the gills, with rubbery knees, and the heavens still spinning crazily about them, they recounted, in awed tones, to their buddies of how, once away from terra firma, their quiet and unassuming pilot had been transformed into a veritable dare-devil—looping, side-slipping, roaring perpendicularly skyward like a rocket, then yanking the joy-stick and plunging with frightening celerity and bullet-like directness straight towards the earth. Of how he had looped-the-loop, and put the ship through still more fantastic and terror-provoking evolutions. Few had been beguiled into sharing a second demonstration of May's prowess in the air. Some even called it a "misguided sense of humour"!

By the end of the war, May had acquired credit for thirteen enemy aircraft shot down, in addition to five not fully confirmed, and sailed back to Canada, gazetted as a Captain, with two wound stripes and the Distinguished Flying Cross.

There were others, too, beside "Wop," who had fought in the skies over France and were headed back towards the shores of Canada. Over a decade later "Wop" was to again meet "Con" Farrell, Walter Gilbert, "Andy" Cruickshank and a host of former war-birds engaged in a different but equally hazardous and exacting fight—the fight to beat down the age-old barriers of the Northland's isolation and gain supremacy over the Arctic skies, the rock-bound lakes and rivers of the Silent Places, and the almost untrodden, and unmapped, Barren Lands.

3

SLEIGH-BOARD PROP

When Theodore Link, Imperial Oil Company geologist, brought in an oil-gusher in the summer of 1920 at the Discovery Well some fifty miles down-river from the lonely outpost of Fort Norman, perched precariously on the river-bank eleven hundred miles beyond the end-of-steel, it did not occasion any great surprise to Northerners. For years, Captain Mills had pointed out the oil-slick on the river to passengers on the Hudson's Bay Company's sternwheeler. In 1789, Alexander Mackenzie made a similar report on his voyage of discovery down the great river that bears his name, whilst other evidences had been noticed still further down-river, and along the Arctic coast. However, when word of the discovery of "black gold" in the Northwest Territories reached Edmonton late that fall it created unusual excitement, and the adventurous from all walks of life prepared to make an assault upon the North in order to get in at the killing.

Whilst no one realized it at the time, it was, actually, the prelude to the famed one-hundred-and-thirty-million dollar United States-sponsored Canol Project which blossomed forth during the Second Great War with an overland pipe-line from Fort Norman to the hastily-erected refinery at Whitehorse, Yukon Territory.

By the time the rivers were frozen the oil rush was in full swing, and an in-rush of would-be oil-stakers commenced to wend their way northward for this frozen Land of Hope. As they mushed down-river, foot-sore, and inadequately equipped to battle with the piled-up *bordeaux* of river ice, the deep snows and the biting cold of fifty and sixty below zero, excitement spread in their wake. If this motley horde of mixed Canadians, Jews, Assyrians, and others, were willing to make this arduous trek for the sake of staking out oil claims there must, indeed, be something to it!

As the invading army of oil-seekers, led by Billy George of Edmonton—self-styled "Empire Builder"—trekked northward there followed an exodus of local residents and trappers from every fort along the route: Peter Baker from Fort Fitzgerald with his dilapidated dog-team; the Connibear party from Fort Smith; Jim Darwish from Fort Rae; Flynn Harris, Indian Agent and Magistrate from Fort

Simpson and his entourage; "Slim" Rader, "Slim" Behn; "Rags" Wilson, and Corporal Bill Doak of the Mounted Police, from Fort Norman along with many others. Not the least conspicuous was Wada, the colourful and mysterious Jap, with his magnificent team of white-haired, sharp-eared huskies. Of a dramatic frame of mind, Wada attired himself to match his team, sporting a *parka* of snow-white mountain goat-skin, white trousers, white winter *mukluks,* and a pair of white polar bear-skin mittens suspended from his neck with a bright worsted cord which matched its myriad colours with the gay embroidery on his dog-*tapis.*[1]

Unprepared for this unexpected demand upon the resources of the trading posts along the river, frozen fish for dog-feed was soon at a premium. But that didn't deter the redoubtable Wada—who seemed to take even greater care of his dogs than of himself. When nothing else was available, he would buy a case of canned salmon—at *two dollars a tin*—rather than see his huskies go hungry!

Food, too, became almost worth its weight in gold, and had to be rationed out to make the supplies last, and many of those oil-seekers knew what it was to go hungry. Old-timers still recall the starved and emaciated Jew who, upon reaching Fort Simpson, vainly sought sustenance for himself and fish for his dog-team. Father Decoux, at the Mission, assured him there was not a fish to spare. "But, Father," he wrung his hands in supplication, "you *must* let me have *something.* You can't turn me down," he moaned. "I'm a good Catholic—a good Catholic. *My father was a priest, and my mother was a nun!*"

Meanwhile Charlie Taylor, Imperial Oil Company representative in Edmonton, gazed with alarm upon this in-rush to take advantage of Link's discovery and blanket the entire area with stakings long before the firm could get into the country at open water. Furthermore, the location of the discovery was considered too remote from civilization to be of any commercial value in view of the inadequate transportation facilities. Faced by these twin problems, he adopted the novel idea of persuading his head office to authorize the purchase of a couple of

---

1. The author also made the trip to Fort Norman to stake oil-claims.

First flying expedition to Mackenzie River District from Edmonton, Alberta, 1921.
Glenbow Archives NA-2303-1

aircraft in order to get his men to Fort Norman long before the spring break-up would permit them to travel north by canoe or sternwheeler and link the new oil-field with civilization.

Inquiries disclosed that a New York firm had obtained the Junkers agency for this continent, and that several of these machines were available. Selection centred on two, all-metal monoplanes—of the type known as J. L. 6's—with cabins capable of accommodating six passengers, and a wing-spread of forty-eight feet. Equipped with engines geared to 175 h.p., they were capable of a maximum speed of 130 miles per hour. These planes could be equipped with pontoons for landing on water, or skis for winter work. Two of these machines, manufactured in New York, had already proven their serviceability in carrying mails between Omaha and San Francisco.

The question of pilots to make the long, mid-winter flight in bring-ing the planes from New York to Edmonton was quickly settled. Since his return from overseas, "Wop" May, with his brother Court, and Lieutenant George W. Gorman, had organized a flying company with one plane, the *City of Edmonton*, with which they had engaged in barn-storming all over the West, especially at fairs and stampedes. Promptly, "Wop" and Gorman were engaged as pilots, while Pete Derbyshire—who had oiled and serviced the *City of Edmonton* at every village and town in Alberta where May and Gorman had put on their flying stunts—consented to go along as engineer.

Towards the end of November, 1920, the party entrained for New York and, in the third week in December, the two, wheel-equipped Junkers took off to wing their way across the continent in a tough, cold air-route which carried them from Belfontaine to Sandusky, Cleveland and Chicago, and on by way of Minneapolis, Brandon and Saskatoon to Edmonton. May's machine bore the Canadian registra-tion, G-CADP, and Gorman's, G-CADQ. Bitter cold, zero visibility and heavy icing forced both planes down at Virden, Manitoba, causing Gorman to remain there several weeks until the damaged tail of his machine was repaired.

For three days, Edmonton had been on tip-toe—waiting to fittingly welcome the intrepid aviators back from their cross-continental flight in the bitterest winter weather—when Court received a long-distance message from "Wop" at Saskatoon advising him of Gorman's accident, and saying that, while bad weather there had held him up, he expected to reach Edmonton around three in the afternoon. But they had not counted on the difficulties experienced in de-icing, and getting oiled-up in the bitter cold, and by the time they took to the air the following-wind had changed to dead ahead. For the last hour of the flight "Wop" gave the machine all she had and, at 5.20 p.m., January 5th, the Junkers, barely visible to the assembled reception party in the rapidly-darkening sky, slipped to the runway beside the May-Gorman hangar and four half-frozen men staggered from the metal cabin.

Early in the afternoon, "Wop's" parents had accompanied Court to the airfield along with Mayor Duggan, Alderman Collison and Charlie Taylor. There a colourful link with the Old and the New was forged by the presence of Frank Oliver, editor and owner of *The Bulletin*, and former Minister of the Interior, who had piloted his own conveyance into Edmonton many years before—not a modern, cabined mono-plane but a primitive, squeaking Red River cart hauled by slow-moving oxen!

"We're mighty glad to see you home, 'Wop,'" beamed the Mayor.

"Maybe *I'm* not glad to get here!" he answered through chattering teeth!

The piloting of the all-metal airships from New York to Edmonton in the middle of winter (commented *The Bulletin*, under date of January 6th, 1921) opens up unthought of vistas in the world of aviation, and the fact that this has been accomplished by Edmonton boys reflects exceptional honour on the city that for many years was the end-of-steel. In the earlier years of railroads, if you wanted to go further than Edmonton, you went by "bull-team" or canoe. Now Captain May has opened up a scheme of transportation that requires neither paved roads nor steel rails.

Here, "Wop" severed his connection with the venture to carry on with his own flying company—May Airlines, Limited—with the remark that his immediate ambition was to "sleep for a week." Lieutenant Elmer G. Fullerton was engaged to take his place along with an extra mechanic, William Hill.

The Junkers were next flown north to Peace River Crossing, where a landing site, a hangar and living quarters were established. The engines were given a thorough overhauling by Derbyshire and Hill and, as weather of Arctic severity continued to prevail, the wheels were replaced by skis, and everything readied for the take-off. With Lieutenant Gorman in command, and an Imperial Oil employee, W. Waddell, as passenger, the expedition headed northward on its historic flight to Fort Norman—carrying sleeping-bags, snowshoes and emergency rations for ten days.

While the Imperial Oil Company was preparing for this new, aerial, assault upon the North I had been busy making my usual winter inspection of the Hudson's Bay Company's fur-trading posts along the Mackenzie River. Just a few days before Fullerton and Gorman were due to take-off for Fort Norman, John Robillard, my Chipewyan guide, drove my dog-drawn *carriole* into the snow-filled courtyard of Fort Simpson. From then on dog-team travel would, of course, be a thing of the past, and the long, tiresome "in between" season of disintegrating ice would set in until the arrival of the stern-wheeled *Mackenzie River* early in July would link us, once again, with the Outside, bringing belated mail, supplies and badly-needed provisions for our depleted larders.

Word had reached back to us at Fort Simpson that Sergeant "Nitchie" Thorne of the Mounted Police, who had headed south by dog-team in February, had delivered his prisoner, Albert Lebeau— accused of murdering his squaw—to Inspector Fletcher at Fort Fitzgerald, and gone on south to Edmonton. There would be no chance, therefore, for "Nitchie" to return until July, when the ice had cleared from Great Slave Lake.

A couple of days after my return—on March 28th—a deafening clamour arose from the courtyard and a crowd of thoroughly frightened Indians hurtled into the trading store. "*The Thunder Bird! The*

Thunder Bird!" they cried, their coppery faces pale beneath the tan of the spring sun. Factor Camsell and I spilled out into the courtyard, wondering what the upset was all about.

"THE THUNDER BIRD!" shrieked another frightened Slavey as he pointed a trembling finger to the sky.

There, to our complete amazement, were two glittering aeroplanes zooming in a wide circle far overhead. Not a soul in Fort Simpson had ever seen an aeroplane! Now, they looked with increasing wonderment at these two mechanical monsters preparing to make a landing.

As the Junkers zoomed down from the skies, dark figures tumbled from the Indian cabins. Here, indeed, was the awesome "Thunder Bird" in person—the holy bird that sits aloft on the highest mountains, hatching out the lightning and making thunder with the drumming of its wings. Yes! here it was—roaring down menacingly—its huge "eyes" flashing in the sunlight.

It was altogether too much! With a hoarse croak of terror, old Chippesaw, the medicine man, plunged back into his cabin, snatched up a muzzle-loader, and dashed outside in time to take a flying shot at the foremost plane before it straightened out and swerved towards him. Throwing away his gun, he dashed, headlong, for the protecting woods—a score of terror-stricken bucks and squaws at his heels.

Gliding over the roofs of the Mission buildings, the foremost Junkers alighted gracefully upon the snow. The skis commenced to skim the drifted surface. The weight settled down upon them. For a brief moment the plane rocked, as though tossed upon billowing waves, then sprawled forward, swayed from side to side, and nose-dived into the hard drifts. There was a sound of rending metal, accompanied by a cascade of glittering crystal. The door flew open and three kicking, sprawling, humans landed, head-first, in the snow. To the utter astonishment of all around, there emerged from the smother the surprised face and lanky form of Sergeant "Nitchie" Thorne! Staggering to his feet, he brushed the snow from his clothing and turned—to look into the amazed eyes of his wife.

Fullerton's machine, noticing the mishap, circled, and alighted without any trouble in the nearby "snye."

32

Captain Gorman swore lustily as he staggered through the drifts towards the damaged machine, which lay like a sick bird upon the snow. A hasty examination disclosed that the prop was completely shattered, the undercarriage wrecked and the wing-tip damaged.

Back at my headquarters at the Hudson's Bay fort, we learned from Gorman the circumstances that had led to the Sergeant's serio-comic return. Just as the fliers were about to leave Edmonton, Sergeant Thorne had run across Captain Gorman. Could the Sergeant, Gorman asked, give him some information concerning ice conditions, and prospective landing places, in the North? The Sergeant did! Then, the thought occurred to Thorne that to return home in *eight hours*—over a route which, ordinarily, took eight long weeks of hard slogging by snowshoe and dog-team—would be accomplishing something unusual and spectacular. The deal was closed, and the Sergeant proceeded north beside Gorman in the cockpit on what was actually the first air-patrol in the history of the Mounted Police, while Dominion Land Surveyor W. Waddell accompanied Elmer Fullerton.

There was just a touch of the dramatic in the Sergeant's make-up, and he'd had reasons of his own for pointing out that Mission field as a prospective landing place instead of the nearby channel between the island and the mainland. Beside the field were the red-roofed buildings of his barracks. It would be quite a joke to make a grandstand landing at his own back door!

With DQ out of commission it was decided that Elmer Fullerton should complete the three-hundred-and-fifty mile flight to Fort Norman the following day. Since, however, Fullerton's machine had developed engine trouble, his propeller and one of his skis were fitted to the damaged plane, and the wing-tip straightened. Next morning, with Hill, Waddell and the equipment aboard DQ, Gorman proceeded to take-off. But ill-luck continued to dog him. As his machine sped forward it rocked, nose-dived, and shivered the second propeller to atoms.

Dolefully, the party returned to the fort, Gorman striding like a caged lion up and down the Mess room, his future plans completely shot by the double disaster. Here they were, he raved, marooned in the wilderness, with not a chance to get out to civilization till the river steamer called on its up-river trip late in July. If they could only get another prop! But, the nearest telegraph office was almost a thousand miles to the southward—there were no radios in those days—while dog-team travel was out of the question as the ice was getting bad. Disconsolately, they made their way to the Mission and hired a cabin from Father Decoux.

Around the Carron stove in the Company's Mess Room that night the aeroplanes became the sole topic of conversation between Fred Camsell, Walter Johnson and others, the rather doubtful performance of these machines having convinced them that you couldn't beat the old, reliable canoe and dog-team. To these insular Northerners the aeroplane was just another of those "contraptions" which, while they might have their place in the effete Outside beyond the frontier, had no place in the North. The fact that Thorne had actually accomplished in eight hours a journey that usually occupied eight weeks of soul-searing toil meant just exactly nothing since the party was now marooned by the failure of their machines. There was, however, one dissenting voice. It was that of Walter Johnson, general handyman around the post in winter, and engineer aboard the diminutive *Liard River* in the summer, who, in his earlier years, had been apprenticed as a cabinetmaker in England.

Until the small hours of the morning, Gorman, Walter and I talked the situation over. "Wouldn't it be possible," I suggested finally, "to make another propeller?"

"I don't think," Walter replied with a quiet smile, "it should be so hard to make one after all."

Fred Camsell chuckled. Elmer Fullerton laughed outright. But, Walter was not to be deterred. Fixing them with a baleful look, he grunted: "I've never yet seen a wood-working job I *couldn't* handle!"

Next morning I persuaded Gorman to accompany Walter and myself to the scene of the mishap, where Walter examined the broken prop minutely. It was composed of nine laminated strips of black walnut glued into a solid block, cut to shape by the most accurate machinery, then finished off by trained workmen and tipped with copper.

"Well, Walter," I queried, "what's the verdict?"

"I dunno." He gave me a long, reflective look. "If only I had the proper kind of wood I still believe I could make one!"

"How about using those oak sleigh-boards I had shipped in last fall to make a dog-*carriole* with?" I suggested. "They're all straight-grained, for I selected them myself, and we've lots of moose-parchments in the fur loft that could be boiled down into glue."

The sleigh-boards were a factory-made product shipped by the Hudson's Bay Company to many of their Northern posts to be steamed and bent into the conventional freight toboggans. They consisted of machine-planed, straight-grained oak boards, twelve feet in length, eight inches wide and one inch in thickness. Later, reports stated that the marooned aviators had hied themselves into the woods, shot a moose and converted the *fresh* skin into glue. *Nothing* could be further from the facts. Owing to the country having been burned over, there were *no* moose anywhere in the vicinity of Fort Simpson that winter, as we knew to our cost—having been forced to subsist all that season on bannock, and hung whitefish which smelled to high heaven, having become thoroughly rotten due to a thaw while they were being transported by scow from the fall fishery at Wrigley Harbour to the fort. Later, the writer, personally, selected the moose-parchments from a number of old, dried skins stored in one of the buildings, and supplied the type considered most suitable for the purpose of making glue.

Gorman shook his head, though I noticed that Walter was intrigued with my suggestion. Examining the pitch of the propeller, he took some measurements.

"How about letting me off for a few days?" he asked. "I'd like to see what I can do."

"Go to it," I said. "Take all the time you like."

To the aviators, the idea of a sleigh-board moose-glue prop seemed ridiculous. Only Hill, Gorman's mechanic, greeted the suggestion with the faintest display of grudging enthusiasm.

A few steamer clamps, an auger, a ship's adze, axes, chisels, planes and crooked knives were the only tools available, yet, quite undaunted,

Walter went ahead. Day by day he sawed and chipped at the toboggan boards. With Hill's assistance, numerous templates of tin were cut to shape, using one unbroken blade as a guide. Gradually the home-made propeller assumed the regulation form and shape. But would it, when completed, be capable of standing a strain of fifteen-hundred revolutions per minute from a 175 h.p. engine? And—would it be capable of driving a machine, weighing two tons, through the air at a speed of ninety miles an hour? Walter, still optimistic, swore it *would!* Everybody else was either sceptical or downright disbelieving.

Meanwhile, Fullerton, Derbyshire and Waddell had overhauled DP's motor, and repaired the damaged skis—the first aircraft repair job ever undertaken in the North. On April 15th, Fullerton adjusted the scarlet-painted, moose-glued sleigh-board prop to G-CADP and climbed into the cockpit. Slowly he opened the throttle until the Junkers was struggling at the restraining ropes, and the new prop swirling fine clouds of snow into the air. With a grim nod, he signalled to us to release the ropes. Again the engine barked out its full power, the staccato detonations from the exhaust shattering the sub-Arctic stillness.

Breathlessly, we watched it roar away, partly obscured by the flying mist of snow, until it appeared in full flight above the sentinel pines.

We stood there, apprehensively watching Fullerton circling for altitude, the sunlight flashing and glinting from the home-made blur in front of the nose. The cadence of its revolutions came down to us in a rising and falling rhythm of sound. Would the prop suddenly disintegrate, and send both ship and pilot crashing to the frozen earth? I glanced at Gorman. Pale and tense, he stood there—the knuckles of his clenched hands white with the force of his grip as he watched the Junkers soar in ever-widening circles.

For nearly an hour, Fullerton put the ship through her paces. Nervous at first, Walter grinned delightedly as the smooth pulsation of the sleigh-board prop continued to purr down from a height of 2,000 feet, or more.

At last the Junkers circled and skimmed in for a landing, this time— *not* on the bumpy Mission field but on the level ice of the snye behind the fort. Fullerton was exultant. The new prop had responded as though it had been turned out on a factory lathe!

I had repeatedly warned Captain Gorman that the Indians reported the prospect of an early break-up of the Liard River. Lulled, however, into a sense of false security by Sergeant Thorne's assurance that the Liard never went out till the month of May, it was not till eight days had elapsed that preparations were completed for the take-off for Peace River Crossing, four hundred miles to the south-west. Already the Liard was showing ominous signs of breaking up. The ice was getting black in spots, and there were distant and ominous rumblings. Meanwhile, the ship had been staked out behind the island where the Liard and Mackenzie meet.

Their preparations at last completed, Gorman and Fullerton crawled into their blankets at the Mounted Police barracks, prepared for a good night's rest. At five o'clock next morning we were awakened at the post by an unholy racket downstairs. Rushing down, we found a half-breed, Henry Lafferty, in a state of wild excitement.

"De Liard Ribber—he's goin' out!" he cried. "De ice—he's pilin' up. De water's risin' fas'!"

Ominous news, indeed. When the swift-flowing Liard River broke up, and hurled its mighty force against the still solid ice of the Mackenzie, it was one of the sights of the North since it was no unusual thing for the river to rise twenty feet in as many minutes, whilst the impact of the crushing, grinding ice against the barrier of the Mackenzie was terrific, and beggared description.

Tearing down to the barracks, we surprised Gorman and his party in bed, awakened them, and all streaked down through the bush to see if the plane was still there, or if it had already been demolished. It was intact—but only about 400 feet of solid ice remained for a take-off— while a foot of muddy water was already swirling above the skis.

With desperate haste we piled the stuff aboard as Fullerton feverishly warmed up the engine. Any moment now might see the ice barrier break, and witness the complete demolition of the plane. Higher and higher crept the turgid flood. Shorter and shorter became the runway. We could hear the deafening roar of the ice as it piled remorselessly into the mouth of the channel.

"Load's too heavy!" Fullerton started pitching the baggage ashore. "I'll have to go alone. Bring that stuff out to the little lake just west of here. I'll wait for you there!"

Next moment he'd given her the gun and was streaking down the snye. To us it seemed that the plane would never rise. She cleared the ice barrier by a scant few inches. Her skis struck open water, sending aloft a shower of glittering spray. Gorman groaned. A slip-up now spelled certain death!

Beneath the ship surged thousands of tons of grinding, roaring ice. Suddenly the plane commenced to climb. We could see a thin, blue line of sky between her and the rising mass of hurtling ice. There arose a choking gasp of relief. She circled, and disappeared above the spiked pines to the westward!

"Look!" cried Walter, his voice tense.

At the foot of the bank, where the ship had been resting but a few brief moments before, roared a mighty, turgid flood, tossing in its grip colossal masses of ice as though they were mere snowballs. Silently, we re-traced our way back to the fort.

Late that evening, when the channel cleared, we ferried Gorman, the two mechanics and Jack Cameron, their guide, across in a canoe and watched them climb the wooded bank with the baggage on their backs. Walter decided to accompany them as far as the little lake where Fullerton intended to set down the plane on solid ice.

Not till late the following day did Cameron and Walter return. They'd found the plane at the appointed spot. The boys had piled aboard, and the ship, with its whirring sleigh-board prop, had disappeared over the silent wilderness, heading into the south-west.

From that time on we speculated and wondered. Had they succeeded in making Peace River Crossing? Or—had they fallen in the unpopulated wilderness across which their route would lie, sacrificing their lives in attempting to introduce the aeroplane to a region which still looked upon the canoe and dog-team as the only practicable modes of travel?

On July 5th, the S.S. *Mackenzie River* churned into Fort Simpson with fluttering pennants and ringing signal bells. Then, for the first time, we learned the outcome of that epic flight from the sub-Arctic fastnesses. The sleigh-board moose-glue prop had fulfilled Walter Johnson's brightest expectations. Four hours after leaving Fort Simpson, Fullerton had set his ship down safely on the frozen surface of Bear Lake near the frontier settlement of Peace River Crossing, and, a few days later, the Hudson's Bay Company's head office in Winnipeg received *the first air mail from the North*—which included my official report of Walter's miraculous feat—mail which I had handed to Gorman on the eve of his departure and which, ordinarily, would not have reached civilization until late the following August!

It was then that I learned, too, of the bitter controversy that had originated, after the party reached Edmonton, as to the construction of the historic propeller.

Hardly had Gorman's party reached there than they were overwhelmed by enthusiastic reporters who told, with banner headlines, how the marooned fliers had risen nobly to the occasion by "hacking a propellor out of birch trees . . . shooting a moose, and converting the skin into glue—and thus mastering a decidedly unpleasant situation." Not a word was mentioned about Walter Johnson, or the part he and the Hudson's Bay Company had contributed to the success of the occasion!

Next day the *Winnipeg Tribune* came out with a totally different story of the events surrounding the construction of the moose-glue prop.

While organizing, and directing, the Hudson's Bay Company's 250th Anniversary Pageant in Winnipeg the previous spring, I had suggested to Sir Robert Kindersley, the Governor, the founding of a staff magazine to help restore the Company's *esprit de corps*—which had been somewhat adversely affected by the invasion of the million-dollar Lamson and Hubbard Company into the North. As a consequence, *The Beaver* magazine came into being, under the editorship of Mr. Thomas. As northernmost correspondent for this magazine, I had sent, by Captain Gorman, a detailed account of the entire episode, giving Walter full credit for his ingenuity and brilliance—little thinking of the storm of protest these *facts* would arouse when Mr. Thomas handed it over to *The Tribune* as a topical news item, along with my original photographs, taken on the spot, or that Walter's accomplishment would be stoutly and acrimoniously denied by some who knew better, and should have been only too pleased to acknowledge his help.

In every way, aviation had gotten off to a poor start so far as the Mackenzie River country was concerned. Not until 1928 were aeroplanes again to penetrate these vastnesses. In the meantime, old-timers returned placidly, and with a distinct measure of relief, to the traditional dog-team, snowshoes and canoe.

4

THE
FLEDGLINGS

Hudson's Bay Company post, Fort Chipewyan, Alberta, ca. Pre 1921.
Glenbow Archives NA-2750-1

M embers of the overseas Flying Corps, returning from France to Canada, scattered to their homes across the Dominion only to find that, though fully trained pilots, who had survived the acid test of war, they had come back to a country where there was no flying to be done. For once, even the most experienced airman discovered to his chagrin that he fitted nowhere into the scheme of things and was, in fact, even less useful on the labour market than the lowliest worker who had toiled all his life with his hands. Having been steeped in a fellowship of danger and the camaraderie of the Mess, with spine-tingling excitement their daily fare, they found themselves cast like waifs on unfriendly and unsympathetic shores. Returned heroes of a day, they were quickly relegated to the obscurity of modern commercialism which, with regrettable lack of vision, saw no place for aviators or planes in the scheme of things now that the Huns were defeated, and war appeared to be a thing of the past.

The necessity of earning daily bread converted some of these erstwhile fliers, whose tunics sported colourful and honoured decorations, into taxi-drivers; others to the uninspiring work of overalled garage-men, while still others were glad to pick up any kind of a labouring job that persistent searching turned up. But the desire to fly was not to be indefinitely restrained by these heart-breaking setbacks. All across Canada were those pockets of restless but unorganized former Air Force pilots living over, whenever they met, the hectic days that now seemed so far away. It remained for Walter Gilbert, who had returned from the Front with few decorations but a vast amount of flying skill, to organize the first group in what was to become a Dominion-wide organization which became directly responsible for most of the present commercial, and much of the subsequent, flying development. Although, after the war, a number of inchoate air organizations, such as the May Brothers one-plane company in Edmonton, came into existence they were doomed to an early demise since they were formed with inadequate capital, and without any definite plan or aim for the future. By 1923 a number of experienced ex-Flying Corps pilots gravitated to Vancouver and met in an attempt to arrange some kind of organization which might serve to perpetuate the common interest in aviation which had been established during the war. Most of them were pretty hard up. The membership was polyglot, indeed, comprising ex-war pilots from the German and Italian air services together with French, American and British fliers. The first club was rightfully dubbed "The International Air Force," of which the president and leading spirit was Walter Gilbert who was destined, later, along with "Wop" May and many others, to become one of the outstanding northern bush pilots.

Learning of the existence of this enthusiastic but poorly-financed club gave Squadron Leader Earl Godfrey, then commanding the Royal Canadian Air Force Air Station at Jericho Beach, Vancouver, an idea which finally emerged in the formation of the Air Force Club of British Columbia. In April of that year he mailed invitations to all flying men to attend a "Flying Service Re-union Dinner and Sunday Air Meet" at the beach. The attendance surpassed all expectations, and bespoke the latent enthusiasm of these former war-birds. Names and addresses were registered, and the International Air Force was merged in the new Air Force of British Columbia under the presidency of Major A. D. Bell-Irving, M.C.

The Club thrived. Its many activities included lectures by club members and prominent visitors, and radio talks by Major D. R. Maclaren and Captain Leonard Miller with a view to creating popular interest in aviation.

From this small and inauspicious beginning developed the great training scheme known as the Canadian Flying Clubs Association, which made a striking contribution to Commonwealth defence by providing Canadian-trained pilots for service in both the Royal Canadian Air Force and the Royal Air Force both in England and the Near East.

Meanwhile, commercial flying was emerging from its chrysalis at Sioux Lookout where, in the days of tribal warfare, Ojibways from nearby Lac Seul ensconced themselves on the lofty rock overlooking the forests to keep watch and ward against invading Sioux war parties. Having staked, and sold, their mining claims in the newly-discovered Red Lake mining area west of Lac Seul, and north of the Canadian

National Railway, H. A. "Doc" Oaks, who might be justifiably acknowledged as the true pioneer of commercial flying, G. A. ("Tommy") Thompson, and S. A. Sammy Tomlinson—that mighty human atom whose knowledge of the North extends from Montreal to the most distant points of the Arctic—pooled their resources in a Curtiss Lark aeroplane, forerunner of the Western Canada Airways. Organizing as Patricia Airways, they started to fly a regular freight and passenger service in the summer of 1926. The vast, flat, forested region bejewelled with countless sparkling lakes made ideal terrain for pontoon-equipped planes and, before long, the Curtiss Lark was successfully shuffling mining equipment, supplies, passengers—and even furs—between Sioux Lookout and Red Lake, Woman Lake, Pine Ridge—as the original Hudson's Bay Company outpost was named, being later changed to Gold Pines—and Buck Lake. Later, as the Pickle Crow mining area developed east of the old Root Portage canoe route[1] and north of the Hudson's Bay post of Osnaburg, the service was extended to include this area.

Since winter strikes both hard and fast in this section of Northern Ontario, and frozen lakes serve as excellent landing places, there was no long "in-between" season to contend with, as in the land of swift-flowing rivers, and it was no trick to discard summer pontoons for winter skis. Even the conservative Hudson's Bay Company was glad to take advantage of this new aerial service by discarding slow-moving Lac Seul freight canoes in favour of sending rush consignments to English River and Albany River trading posts by plane.

Every trip disclosed new and unheard of advantages to be derived through the initiative of "Doc" Oaks, Tommy Thompson and the ever-faithful but explosive Sammy which converted that small section of the North towards an air-mindedness that was to spread by leaps and bounds, and herald the last phase in the picturesque Fur Trade that had long dominated the lakes and forests.

Having demonstrated the efficacy of their pint-sized air company, "Doc" Oaks, Sammy Tomlinson, and Al Cheesman of Antarctic fame,

---

1. The writer re-organized the Hudson's Bay Company's Lac Seul to Osnaburg canoe transport in the summer of 1914.

decided to approach James A. Richardson, Winnipeg business man, and member of the Hudson's Bay Company's Canadian Committee, with a much more ambitious project. Events that were to influence the whole of industrial life, and revolutionize the Far North with its eternal distance and frost barriers, were in the making! In fact, the first ground-work had already been laid for the vast air-transportation system which was to do so much to develop the North and encourage intensive mining activity, and make household words of such names as "Doc" Oaks, Al Cheesman, "Punch" Dickins, "Wop" May, Bill Broatch, "Con" Farrell, Walter Gilbert and many other future bush fliers who had received their initial training on the battlefields of France. Capital was all that "Doc" needed to create a Canada-wide organization whose wings would cast their shadows from the Great Lakes to the snow igloos of the "Blonde" Eskimos on Canada's Arctic foreshore.

A Westerner of generosity and vision who, despite his millions, was easy of approach, James Richardson's quick mind promptly foresaw the vast potentialities in the creation of a network of fast-speeding aeroplanes reaching out from the end-of-steel into the barely-scratched and little-known mineral storehouse of the Pre-Cambrian Shield. With the time factor all but eliminated by the speed of aerial flight for transportation of equipment, men and supplies to new mineral areas, the scope of mining development might be advanced by tens of years in point of time, the output proportionately increased, and the wealth of Canada brought to a new high.

"Doc's" faith in the astuteness of Manitoba's magnate proved to be more than justified. In December, 1926, the Western Canada Airways came into being, and three Fokker airplanes: the *Fort Churchill*, the *City of Winnipeg* and the *City of Toronto* duly put in an appearance at Sioux Lookout, which continued to grow by leaps and bounds as an air base—with a subsidiary base at Hudson on Lost Lake, fourteen miles to the westward.

While the pioneer Patricia Airways continued to operate under the management of Dale Atkinson, with Captain Ross at the controls of the Curtiss Lark, this lone eagle of the skies now shared its labours with the fleet of powerful Fokkers, and the list of passengers, freight, gold samples, ore, picks, shovels, mining machinery and huskie dogs assumed ever-growing proportions. When Fred Palmer, Port Engineer at Fort Churchill on the storm-tossed shore of Hudson Bay, sent in a rush order to the Government to fly men and freight, including half a ton of dynamite, to this cold and austere spot, Western Canada Airways alone displayed any inclination to tackle what then seemed a decidedly precarious job.

At 9 a.m., on March 27th, 1927, the *City of Winnipeg* and the *City of Toronto* took off from the sub-base at Hudson—the first commercial aircraft to fly over the dreaded Barren Lands. The pilots were Lieutenant Bert Balchen and F. G. Stevenson, after whom Stevenson Field in Winnipeg derives its name, while the chief mechanic was the irrepressible Al Cheesman who, years later, was to assist Sir Hubert Wilkins in his search for the Russian fliers lost in the Arctic. The load was three-quarters of a ton, including sleeping-bags, snowshoes, *parkas*, emergency rations, and fourteen Dominion Government engineers as passengers, to say nothing of the dynamite!

Weather conditions in the vicinity of Fort Churchill are fit for neither man nor beast. The damp cold is more terrible than that of any part of the Arctic. Even at sixty below zero the frigid air is never still, and the paralyzing dampness, penetrating the thickest furs, seems to freeze the very marrow in one's bones. Salty tides, rolling far inland, leave jagged masses of sharp, up-ended ice piled one atop another that are a menace to life and limb, to say nothing of the undercarriage of an airplane.

The route, after hitting the eastern shore of Lake Winnipeg at Berens River, followed the lake north to Norway House, former Hudson's Bay Company's headquarters for Keewatin—Land of the North Wind—thence via Cache Lake to Fort Churchill, in the shadow of old Fort Prince of Wales. The difficulties were numerous. Frigid fogs rolled down from the Bay, retarding visibility. High winds and biting blizzards roared inland, carrying billowing clouds of snow in their wake. At times, a start would be made from Cache Lake in brilliant sunshine only to find the plane fighting the inevitable fog and blizzards within the space of minutes. Skis were constantly succumbing to pressure ridges or broken ice, necessitating long snowshoe journeys to bring repair material. When Stevenson broke the scavenger pipe of his machine while landing at Fort Churchill he succeeded in making temporary repairs, only to make a forced landing a hundred miles from his destination. In this inhospitable Land of Little Sticks, devoid of almost all human habitation—with no worthwhile trees for shelter, and a temperature that caused his breath to freeze on the breast and cowl of his *capote*—he mushed sixty long, frigid miles ere he was fortunate enough to be picked up by a wandering Cree hunter, badly frost-bitten and suffering intensely from cold and privation.

Despite these handicaps, Western Canada Airways came out triumphant. Some twenty-seven round trips of four-hundred air-miles were made from Cache Lake to Fort Churchill, all supplies and equipment being delivered well within the contractual period.

To the world at large the success of these trips was a revelation, not only concerning the almost heroic and resourceful work of the pilots and mechanics but as an indication of the possibilities of large-scale commercial flying. Both the *Free Press* and the *Tribune* of Winnipeg were loud in their praises. Air transport had been subjected to the acid test in the rigorous climate of Hudson Bay and not found wanting, while "all the fliers appeared very unconcerned yet did a marvellous piece of work ... Gone is the mythical barrier to the Far North," wrote a reporter. "With airplanes and radio, we have an easy access to our wonderful mineral belt, extending 2,000 miles in length, the greatest undeveloped mineral area in the world."

The most progressive step in the fast-moving development of commercial flying occurred in March, 1927, when Western Canada Airways was officially incorporated under the Companies Act for the purpose of establishing and maintaining regular aircraft services in the Dominion—to include the carrying of freight, passengers and mail, photographic surveys, and aerial mapping of timber limits. Overnight, as it were, these services became an integral part of everyday life, while business in the mining areas and other parts of the North was already showing signs of acceleration.

When, in June, 1927, the Post Office Department authorized Western Canada Airways to carry mail the first Manitoba Air Mail was inaugurated, but without any Government subsidy, all such mail being carried at ordinary freight rates. Up to this time all mail had been carried into eastern Manitoba mining areas by canoe, or motor-boat, in the summer and by the time-honoured dog-team, or horse-sled, in winter. Immediately, the Winnipeg Mining Bureau arranged for the establishment of three new post offices: one at Wadhope, another at Bissett, and the third at English Brook.

Two months later, Western Canada Airways extended their airmail routes from Winnipeg to Cormorant Lake, northern Manitoba headquarters of the Royal Canadian Air Force. Its fleet of planes continued to increase in number to keep up with the fast-growing demand and recognition of the benefits of air transport. At the end of the first eight months of 1927 they had flown more than a thousand passengers through the skies; 200,000 pounds of freight and equipment; and had covered over 150,000 miles in some 1,500 flying hours, flights having extended over Quebec, Ontario and Manitoba. Up to this time, and until the organization of Commercial Airways in Edmonton, no subsidy or official assistance of any kind whatsoever was provided by the Canadian Government, all development of the air routes in the North, and mining areas of Manitoba and Ontario, having been entirely unassisted.

In June, 1928, Western Canada Airways welcomed to its growing staff another resourceful First War fighter pilot who was to make a name for himself in blazing new air trails from Norway House to the shores of Hudson Bay, and north to the sealing grounds of the primitive "blondie" Eskimos. Born in Smiths Falls, Ontario, with an inherent love of adventure, C. M. G. "Con" Farrell had joined up for the First Great War in the 128th Battalion of Moose Jaw, a raw and underaged recruit. With intuitive foresight, his father, Judge Farrell of Regina, suggested he "smarten up" and transfer to the Royal Flying Corps, a decision that made his future life one long story of thrills and hair-raising adventure, and gave to the North one of its most intrepid and resourceful bush pilots. A twenty-year-old veteran with the blue and white ribbon of the Distinguished Flying Cross, he returned to Canada, intending to settle down to the ordinary routine of a family doctor by way of the University of Manitoba. Fortunately for the history of bush flying, "Con" tossed away his medical books and was next heard of in association with the veterans Bill Spence, Bill Broatch, "Doc" Oaks, "Wop" May, "Punch" Dickins and Walter Gilbert, moving his headquarters as he helped enlarge the activities of Western Canada Airways from Lac du Bonnet to Sioux Lookout, The Pas and Island Falls.

Passengers found "Con" daring and resourceful but gruff at times, and never willing to suffer fools gladly or take unnecessary chances. An overseas buddy and lifelong friend of "Wop" May's, he had his own subtle way of dealing with delinquent Indians he discovered draining-off gasoline from his Company's caches at night. When they complained indignantly to the Mounted Police that their outboard "kickers" refused to kick, and had developed strong traces of sugar in their gas-tanks, "Con" grinned as the discomfited redskins were dismissed with a peremptory warning against surreptitious thefts of gasoline from Company planes or caches.

Meanwhile, Western Canada Airways, looking for an appropriate crest, had, with prophetic vision, picked on the hardy and intelligent Canada goose. Indigenous to the Northland, it was an appropriate emblem, indeed. At the time, however, the great and expanding northern destiny of the organization, and that of many pilots who later served under its emblem, still lay in the future.

Despite Herculean efforts to provide an outlet for his one-plane company, "Wop" May had long since been forced to the realization that entertaining crowds at country fairs, and competing with such carnival characters as the Fat Lady, the Sword Swallower and ebony-coloured "belly-dancers" was a poor foundation upon which to establish his future flying career. Unlike Northern Ontario, where active mining was already in progress within easy aerial reach of the steel, the region to the north of Edmonton remained stagnant so far as actual mining operations were concerned. True, there had been an abortive and short-lived attempt to wrest gold from Caribou Island, while the

Atlas Exploration Company had located vast deposits of zinc and other minerals on Great Slave Lake, but there was still no demand for air transportation to that area. Facing the same frustration which had bedevilled Walter Gilbert and other returned pilots, and deeply depressed by the accidental death of his brother, Court, which had occurred on May 21st the year before from a fall in the Macdonald Hotel, "Wop" had finally disposed of his flying interests to Great Northern Services, Limited, in the summer of 1923.

Romance, meanwhile, had come to "Wop's" aid in assuaging the loss of his flying career. A slim, dark-haired girl from Dayton, Ohio, Violet Brodie, had a passionate love of horses, and an almost uncanny faculty for handling the most refractory steed that had won her many honours at horse shows on both sides of the border and furnished her with a reputation of being one of the most outstanding horse-women and polo players in the West. On November 20, 1924, "Wop" and Vi were married by the Reverend D. G. McQueen in Edmonton.

Hardly had the wedding bells ceased to chime before "Wop" and his bride were on their way to Dayton, where the erstwhile pilot was to engage in less exciting and more prosaic duties with the International Cash Register Company though, in his heart, remained the yearning for the feel of the joystick, the roar of the throttle, and the exhilarating thrill of soaring through the skies.

5

THE CONQUEST
OF THE BARRENS

I t was not until a hot July day in the summer of 1928, seven years after the first wounded Junkers limped back to civilization with its famed moose-glue prop, that another airplane attempted to venture into the fastnesses of the Mackenzie River region. Pierre Mercredi, Hudson's Bay factor at Fort Resolution, overlooking the wide reaches of Great Slave Lake, gazed with apprehensive eyes into the sky as the air seemed to vibrate with strange pulsations, as though a million monster mosquitoes had suddenly taken wing. From a fleecy cloud emerged what appeared at first to be a giant dragonfly, sending the assembled Dog-Ribs and Yellow-Knives ducking for the protection of their conical tepees while Pierre remained rooted to the spot. The "dragonfly" quickly assumed the form of an airplane, circled, and settled like a duck on the mirrored surface of the lake. It was the first airplane Pierre or any of the Indians had ever seen. From the metal cabin emerged a khaki-clad figure who waved his hat while he balanced precariously upon a pontoon, calling loudly for a canoe.

Launching a birchbark, Chittom Houle, the interpreter, pushed out with a couple of scared Dog-Ribs and, a few minutes later, the slim, lithe figure of the redoubtable "Doc" Oaks, with raw-boned Jake Davidson, the impassive Charlie McLeod and a couple of other high-booted, mackinaw-clad prospectors, disembarked upon the beach. In a few words "Doc" informed Pierre that he had left Fort McMurray only about four hours before, a statement Pierre received with obvious and embarrassing disbelief.

"We've just organized the Northern Aerial Minerals Exploration Company in Toronto to comb the North by airplane for mineral prospects," "Doc" informed Pierre. "We're headed for the Nahannie Mountains to look for that lost McLeod Mine, and we've got Charlie McLeod here with us as guide. I'm going to drop the boys as near Dead Man's Valley as possible," he continued. "Leave 'em a grubstake, and that collapsible canoe tied to the plane there . . . let 'em prospect around all summer, then pick 'em up again in the fall."

Purchasing some gasoline and the few articles he needed from the trading post, "Doc" and his entourage headed back to the plane and soon the machine was winging its way towards the saw-toothed

Nahannies of ill-omen in quest of the hidden gold.

The story of the Lost McLeod Mine was a familiar one to every Northerner. Probably the largest unexplored area in the North, the rugged Nahannie Mountains, lying sixty-odd miles west of Fort Simpson at the junction of the Liard and Mackenzie Rivers, were almost inaccessible before the coming of the airplane. For many years fantastic stories had been carried south to civilization by nomad trappers of an alleged tropical valley situated amongst their towering crests, a valley that was said to have escaped the impact of the Ice Age, wherein monsters of a forgotten age were said to disport themselves in warm pools amidst luxuriant tropical vegetation. An Indian named Chequina had added impetus to this story some years before when he informed a party of scientists, whom he was guiding through the Athabasca country, that his father had actually come into contact with a tribe of primitive Indians who had told him of this "Medicine Valley," and vouched for the existence of strange monsters amongst its palm-girt lakes. From his medicine-bag, Chequina had drawn a piece of buckskin upon which one of these Indians had depicted a crude portrayal of one of these creatures, and the scientists gazed in astonishment at the faded outline of a dinosaur. The allure of this story, and the fanciful dream that prehistoric monsters might yet be disporting themselves in this sub-Arctic "medicine valley," had persisted down through the years, having formed the background for more than one colourful story of the Nahannie country.

Somewhere in the vicinity of this alleged valley, Willie and Frank McLeod, sons of Murdoch McLeod, former Hudson's Bay factor at Fort Liard, were murdered back in 1906. At first it was thought that they had succumbed to the bullets of the wild Nahannies of the Mountains. Then their elder brother, Charlie, who was now guiding the "Doc" Oaks party, had trailed their erstwhile partner, Wade, across the Rockies to the Pacific Coast, only to run upon him in a saloon in Vancouver, throwing money around like a drunken sailor. Returning to the North, Charlie traced the route taken by Wade and his brothers, stumbled on their old camp near the Flatt River, and discovered the headless skeletons of Frank and Willie—with sufficient evidence to convince him that they had been murdered in their sleep by their partner—who had decamped with the stake of gold.

It was late in the fall of 1928 when W. John McDonogh of the Northern Aerial Minerals Exploration Company landed his plane in the snye behind Fort Simpson after an abortive attempt to pick up Charlie McLeod and his party, whom "Doc" Oaks had dumped in the Nahannie ranges to search for Dead Man's Valley. Still in his early thirties, the genial and irrepressible McDonogh had learned flying the hard way in war-torn planes over the battlefields of France when only seventeen. Returning to Canada with a wealth of hard-won experience he eventually joined up with "Doc" Oaks. Heading for that devil's playground of majestic peaks and abysmal canyons, which constitute the Nahannie ranges, he found himself circling an undefiled and untrodden wilderness; a land of awe-inspiring vastness inhabited by the grizzly and the moose, the mountain-goat and the big-horn sheep—but not a vestige of a sign did he see in this untrammeled wilderness of the party he sought. He had, however, earned the distinction of becoming the first pilot to fly into the Yukon.

Realizing that it was very much like hunting a needle in a haystack, he had been forced by dwindling fuel supplies to head for the nearest habitable spot—Fort Simpson. After refuelling, and enjoying the genial hospitality of the Hudson's Bay Company's staff, he loaded aboard Mr. Adams, a Seattle mining engineer, and headed southward, where he was soon to establish the Spence-McDonogh Air Company, and help in blazing new air trails over the uncharted wastes of Keewatin—Land of the North Wind.

Hardly had McDonogh departed, when the door of the Master's House flew open and, into the room reeled four animated skeletons in the last stages of exhaustion. Bearded and begrimed, their clothing patched with greasy buckskin, they proved to be Charlie McLeod and the human caricatures who represented the rest of the prospecting party "Doc" had flown into the Nahannies the previous July.

On their flight into the Nahannies, Charlie had doggedly searched for the little lake where he had buried his brothers, intending to use it as a landmark, but his efforts had been in vain. So "Doc" had dumped them somewhere amongst the forbidding peaks with grub, ammunition and a small, collapsible canoe, and had flown back to civilization, promising to pick them up in the fall. Till long after "Doc's" plane was due they had waited, but, as the leaves turned to scarlet, and the grim Nahannies took on the austere garb of approaching winter, they looked with horror on the prospect of being marooned in this desolate and sombre wilderness with all its evil associations.

With only a small side of dried moose meat for rations, they had finally bolted their flimsy canoe together and committed themselves to the turbulent waters of some unnamed stream and hurtled to the southward. At race-horse speed they were swirled along in their cockleshell craft. Rock walls closed in until the serpentine channel, twisting in hairpin turns, was crushed between rock ramparts that reared themselves thousands of feet above them. Onward they swept, cursing "Doc" for his failure to fly them out as they careened over black chutes roaring through narrow chasms so deep that the sky seemed like a mere silver thread in the blackness that engulfed them, the very air vibrating with the roar of angry waters that spattered in their faces and half-blinded them. Warned by the menacing roar of still another cascade, the men managed to scramble ashore—barely in time—and perched precariously on a foam-bespattered ledge as the entire river leapt over a precipice and roared in a foaming torrent, split by a fang-like rock, three hundred feet below.

"All summer we searched for Dead Man's Valley," Charlie told Factor Camsell disgustedly, "but nary a sign did we see. Instead, we ran right into that there 'Tropical Valley' them Injuns talk about!"

The romantic oasis, with its luxurious tropical vegetation, was a myth, Charlie said. Nor were there living mastodons or leathery-winged pterodactyls or creatures of a forgotten age to halt their footsteps. Having climbed a range of verdant hills, they descended into a mist-enshrouded valley about two miles wide and eight miles long. Mud volcanoes arose, sputtering, from grassy bottoms—sending up coils of whitish vapour. Springs of hot, sulphurous water welled up from between the rocks. The air was warm and enervating, and the fern-strewn moss scored with a web of animal trails.

In their rambles they'd stumbled on a tumbled-down cabin, proving that the valley had known at least one human occupant. Before the door was sprawled the headless skeleton of a giant white man. Beside it, overgrown with weeds, lay a broken rifle, the barrel badly bent. But all evidence of his identity had been destroyed by pack-rats, though unused firewood and weathered ax-cuttings indicated that the nameless pioneer had perished at least fifteen years before.

A couple of days later, Charlie and his party boarded the S. S. *Distributor* on her last trip of the season, south towards Fort Smith, glad to find themselves aboard a familiar river-steamer, but still cursing "Doc" and his "damned airplane" for failing to show up.

Meanwhile, still another airplane, this time belonging to the fast-spreading Western Canada Airways, had invaded the Northwest Territories. On September 6th, "Punch" Dickins descended like a winged Mercury from the skies at Fort Smith to gaze with lofty mien upon those lowly mortals whose fate it was to be exiled in these northern wastes. With two American mining men as passengers, he had started from Winnipeg, heading north to Chesterfield Inlet on the dreary shore of Hudson Bay, thence west, by way of the Thelon River, across the heart of the untrodden Barren Lands.

These Barrens, as the vast tundra stretching from the shores of Hudson Bay to the valley of the Mackenzie and north from the Land of Little Sticks to the rim of the Arctic is called, were linked with many tragic stories of cannibalism and starvation. Under the most favourable conditions, crossing these endless, uninhabited moors and sandy eskars meant months and, sometimes, years of arduous travel yet "Punch" had succeeded in conquering their awesome aloofness in perfect comfort in a mere matter of hours! In a little over twenty-seven hours of flying time, he and his party had covered some 3,000 miles in an absence from civilization of less than two weeks. It was justly considered one of the most daring and spectacular flights yet attempted, which was more than emphasized by the tragic news we had received of the death of Jack Hornby and his two companions in the very heart of the region traversed by Dickins. A tragedy that shook the North to its foundations.

C. H. "Punch" Dickins, ca. 1930.
Glenbow Archives NA-1258-37

A recluse and a hermit, a silent wanderer in the frozen, blizzard-swept Barrens, Jack Hornby would disappear in the fall from Fort Resolution, Fort Norman or some other post on the Mackenzie with the slenderest of equipment: a rifle, ammunition, a pack-dog or a canoe, and be swallowed up in the tundra to the eastward. A year, or, perhaps, eighteen months would elapse then he would appear at some post hundreds of miles away—gaunt, unkempt and hungry—with a glossy black beard reaching to his waist. He would camp in one of the cabins, consorting most of the time with the Indians, trade his furs—and disappear again!

Trained for a career in the British Diplomatic Service, he had forsaken everything to live this life of utter loneliness and isolation. Living like an Indian, he poked fun at us fur traders, the Mounted Police and others who had learned by hard experience the value of carrying a well-filled grub-box to tide us over possible emergencies. Twice he'd been saved from starvation by wandering Dog-Ribs, who had brought him into some post barely in the nick of time. Back in the early 'twenties he had persuaded Captain Critchell-Bullock to spend a winter with him in the Barrens. But, Bullock had hardly envisaged spending the bitter winter in an odoriferous wolf-den in the heart of the tundra, and he had been more than glad when he finally reached the Hudson's Bay post at Chesterfield Inlet, even though more dead than alive.

After a trip to England in 1925, Hornby returned to the Barrens with two young, and totally inexperienced, Englishmen—Harold Adelard, a former school teacher, and an eighteen-year old schoolboy, Edgar Christian. Secure in the sense of his own hardihood and ability to live off the country, he had headed for the forks of the Hanbury and the Thelon with equipment confined to the irreducible minimum: guns, ammunition, fish-nets, snaring-twine, and a dangerously low supply of flour and other staples.

Like others, who had lived to regret it, Hornby intended to depend on the great caribou migration for sustenance. Across the Barrens migrated the mighty caribou herds in the spring and fall. Each spring, as the mounting sun dispersed the violet Arctic night, they surged forward like a rolling tide. Leaving the bulls to browse around the treeless tundra, the females struck northward and crossed over to the Arctic islands to do their fawning. In the fall the biological urge would send them back to the mainland, where the bulls would be waiting and, together, they would scamper southward a thousand miles to attain the protection of the scrub timber—the so-called Land of Little Sticks—ere winter blizzards roared relentlessly down from the Pole. For days, for weeks, they would roll across the barren tundra; a palpitating, steaming, seething ocean of animated flesh and fur, a forest of heaving, tossing antlers, the castanet-like clicking of thousands upon thousands of heart-shaped hooves shattering the primeval stillness while, for a day's journey distant, the fetid caribou smell would hang heavily in the air.

There was, however, an unpredictability about their paths of migration since a sudden blizzard might split the herd, causing it to fork off in entirely different directions, while other inexplicable causes would result in there being no caribou one season where there had been countless thousands the year before.

About two months before "Punch" Dickins made his flight across the Barrens a prospecting party, led by Harry Wilson of Colonel MacAlpine's Dominion Explorers, was lazily paddling its grey-painted canoes down the turbulent Thelon some seventy miles from its junction with the Hanbury. It was a hot July day, and the flies were bad. Ahead, a stand of dwarf spruce broke the grey-brown landscape in a patch of verdant green. It was the first sign of sturdy growth they had seen in many a day, and one bronzed paddler lifted his battered felt hat and emitted a delighted whoop. "Look, boys," shouted one of the steersmen, "a cabin in the timber. Must be somebody around!"

Beaching the canoes, the khaki-clad crews leapt ashore, laughing and talking loudly as they straggled through the shade towards the cabin. There was a peculiar exhilaration in being amongst these pines with their spreading boughs after so many days in the open and treeless tundra. Suddenly they came upon a sight that chilled the marrow in their spines. Stretched, full-length, before the cabin door lay two dead men—Jack Hornby and Harold Adelard! Upon a narrow bunk within lay the body of young Christian, the lad who had looked forward with eager anticipation to a life of glamorous adventure in the Barrens!

The pitiful bareness of that little cabin told all too plainly its own tragic story of discouragement and want. The complete absence of caribou skins was in itself significant to men who knew their North. So, too, were those gnawed and polished bones upon the floor. Rifles there were, and ammunition aplenty, but not a scrap of food save a small quantity of tea. The caribou had failed them!

With that perversity that characterized their movements, the caribou had failed to follow their usual course of migration and had not come near the cabin. Day after day, month after month, they had waited in vain for the thunder of countless hooves and the trembling of the earth that would presage the great autumn migration. Then winter, with its awful cold, its biting blizzards and its menace, had swept down upon them with their larder empty and their strength sapped by lack of food. In utter desperation they had dug up old bones and bits of discarded skin and offal thrown out in the fall, gnawed the bones to a polish, and boiled the putrid skins in a vain endeavour to extract even a little nourishment.

In simple, poignant words these last days of suffering were told in the diaries and letters they had left behind them in the cabin. Jack Hornby had died on the night of April 16th, 1927; Harold Adelard two weeks later. To young Christian, Hornby's nephew, death had not been merciful. For weeks he had lived beside the dead bodies of his companions, watching the warm breath of summer revitalizing the Northland; listening to the geese and ducks as they winged by overhead, and seeing caribou browsing in the distance—beyond reach now. Waiting! Waiting! Exhibiting in his ghastly loneliness a magnificent courage which deserved a more fitting reward than an untimely death.

When "Doc" Oaks organized the Northern Aerial Minerals Exploration Company that year in Toronto he displayed a noteworthy aptitude for picking raw material to fill the ranks of the Northland's future bush pilots. John McDonogh, the first of the bush fliers to invade the skies of the Yukon while in search of Dead Man's Valley, and whose name was to loom large in the history of northern aerial pioneering, was only one of the Irishmen "Doc" had hailed from obscurity. Thomas Mayne "Pat" Reid, who had left his home at Ballyrooney in Northern Ireland to join the Royal Naval Air Service in 1915, and won the Distinguished Flying Medal for outstanding service in the First Great War, was won over from the infant Ontario Provincial Air Service at Sault Ste. Marie by "Doc" to blaze the first aerial bush trails from Fort Churchill on the rock-girt shores of Hudson Bay to Chesterfield Inlet in the Barrens, and from Moose Factory in fir-fringed James Bay to the isolation of Port Harrison. This volatile and utterly fearless Irishman, whose restless soul carried him that same summer from Sioux Lookout on a pioneer air-flight over the eternal glaciers and snow-capped peaks of ice-girt Baffin Land, had the doubtful distinction of being the only bush pilot to read his own obituary when he returned unexpectedly to his base at Sioux Lookout when reported missing after a prolonged absence of six weeks.

"Glad I lived to read *this*," he said, his weather-tanned face widening into a mischievous grin as his eyes followed the obituary blurb, penned by Robert McAlpine McGregor, publisher, editor and compositor of Sioux Lookout's one-man newspaper, wherein he presented the supposedly defunct reader as a knight in shining armour fighting a losing fight against the unknown terrors of the Polar spaces. Pat's sparkling eyes sought out Sammy Tomlinson. "I'm sure *some* guy! And—I never even suspected it till I was supposed to have turned up my toes."

In the months to come, with the late Duke Schiller, another noted bush flier, Pat was to spend six months on a twenty-five-thousand mile flight which carried him from the massive ruins of Fort Prince of Wales, overlooking Churchill Harbour, across the Barren Lands to Bathurst Inlet and the Coppermine, in the heart of the Cogmollock sealing grounds, thus completing with his flimsy crate, and under primitive flying conditions, the conquest of the Northwest Passage by air.

When the tired dog-team carrying the first winter mail to the North emerged from a cloud of spinning flakes under the urging of the caribou-hide whip of the skin-clad Indian runner on December 12th, 1928, and pulled up before the diminutive post office at Fort Smith, I received word from the Hudson's Bay Company that Western Canada Airways was preparing an assault upon the isolation of the Northwest Territories, and was organizing a regular passenger and freight service for the Mackenzie River district. It was accompanied by a request that I arrange for appropriate landing places to be marked off at all down-river forts. Local half-breeds were promptly employed levelling off landing places on the Slave River at Fort Fitzgerald, and on the rough river ice beneath the high cutbank at Fort Smith. Meanwhile, I arranged with Captain Bob Hastings of the Royal Canadian Corps of Signals to relay word to the factors at Fort Resolution and Fort Simpson to dispatch Indian couriers by dog-team and snowshoes to notify the other posts down the Mackenzie to have the rough ice levelled off and landing places prepared and brushed with spruce trees so that they could be easily identified from aloft.

The Northwest Territories, into which Western Canada Airways now proposed to extend its activities, had not been discovered by Ottawa until the oil boom of 1920, when the settlement of Fort Smith suddenly found itself projected into the position of becoming the diminutive "capital" of this vast and almost unpopulated wilderness.

In those pre-Abbott days the region did not appear to have any taxable commodities and was, officially, overlooked. But the presence of oil implied other prospective wealth hidden somewhere in its untamed fastnesses. Hard on the heels of this discovery there had arrived at Fort Smith an administrative body to cope with the oil rush, and administer the affairs of the Territories. Headed by stocky, grey-haired Major Lockie Burwash, a veteran of the Yukon and former Assistant Gold Commissioner at Dawson during the palmy days of the gold rush, the party consisted of twenty men, some of whom were accompanied by their wives. But, as sometimes happens in Governmental circles, another and different Ottawa department not so many doors away, considering the country not yet ripe for exploitation, had effectively killed the incipient oil rush by enacting regulations that eliminated the small man from the picture. Thus, when the Major arrived with his cohorts he discovered there was no one to "administer" except a few wandering Indians, half-breeds and fur traders who were very much adverse to being "administered." Smiling, good-natured, and thoroughly capable, the Major was, unquestionably, an asset to the North and eminently fitted for his position as Commissioner of the Territories. But this was more than could be said for many of his staff, mostly young college lads, fine fellows—but entirely out of place in the North. Had the Government searched the land from end to end it could hardly have concocted a more composite hell's broth than that which was soon simmering in this backwoods settlement from the human ingredients sent in.

Realizing that idle hands are apt to get into mischief, the Major turned the boys loose with peevies, axes and cross-cut saws to cut logs for a dwelling to house the party. Howls of fiery protest arose at such menial and unaccustomed labour. Quarrel piled on quarrel until the reverberations of these struggles echoed from Fort McPherson to distant Ottawa.

Gradually there arose in the newly-styled capital of the Territories an ugly, sprawling log building which was honoured with the title *Government House*. Again the fat was in the fire! Mrs. Card, spirited and strong-minded wife of Gerald Card, the Indian Agent, let it be known in no uncertain terms that *her* house was Government House. It had been Government House for years, before any of the Major's party had ever seen the Athabasca—*and Government House it was going to remain!*

With two Government Houses in a settlement comprising a few sprawling Indian cabins, a couple of trading posts and a Mission, and half a dozen cliques all warring with each other, Fort Smith became the subject of ridicule from the end-of-steel to the Polar Sea.

By 1928 mining activity was bringing other changes in its train. Lockie Burwash's log Government House was now occupied by a Mining Recorder, while the former two-man Mounted Police barracks had been enlarged into Headquarters for "G" Division with six dapper

Constables stationed there to the immense delight of the ladies—both red and white. Buffalo rangers rubbed shoulders with red-coated Mounties; moccasined trappers hobnobbed with sun-tanned river-men; dog-drivers in caribou-skin *parkas* made love to Slavey beauties in the lodges, while the white wives of Government officials tripped the trails in high-heeled shoes and fashionable dresses. And, with it all, Fort Smith still suffered from a superiority complex; a complex which dated back to the days when "stuck-up Mrs. LaHache" had owned two enamelled teapots—one for tea and one for coffee! A sign of hopeless ostentation which had been frowned upon by her native sisters, hard-boiled rivermen and *voyageurs* alike, and had given the settlement a bad name which it had never succeeded in living down.

This pseudo-civilization, five hundred miles beyond the frontier, had also brought in its train amusing paradoxes galore, to say nothing of innumerable unique characters who stood out with startling clar-ity, their idiosyncrasies bared to the world by that utter and disturb-ing lack of privacy which characterizes life in the wide open spaces.

Newcomers to the country stood aghast at the immensity of the almost unpeopled region that swept northward to the shadow of the Pole. Already they had travelled six hundred miles out of Edmonton, with primeval wilderness about them on every hand. Now, at Fort Smith, situated two miles north of the 60th parallel, they found they were only on the threshold of a still vaster wilderness, the Northwest Territories. A million and a quarter square miles in extent, it reached in magnificent isolation eastward to the eternal glaciers of ice-girt Baffin Land; westward to the Rocky Mountains and Alaska's saw-toothed Endicotts, and northward beyond the mist-enshrouded Arctic archipelago to the very Pole itself. A region one-third the size of the United States that, in 1932, boasted a population of 9,733 souls, com-prising 4,056 Indians, 4,670 Eskimos, and 1,007 white traders, trap-pers, priests, missionaries, Mounted Police and Government officials.

Along its northern rim, living in a modern Stone Age, dwelling in dome-shaped igloos lighted with flickering blubber-lamps of stone, fur-clad Eskimos hunted the caribou, the polar bear and white fox, and harpooned the whale and walrus as did their ancestors before the white man came. In the forests fringing the Mackenzie and its tributaries skin-clad Dog-Ribs, Chipewyans and Indians of a dozen tribes toiled on snowshoes through the silvered aisles of snow-mushroomed forests in quest of the pelts of beaver, lynx and silver fox which they bartered with the factors at the isolated trading posts. Here, too, scarlet-coated men of the Mounted Police sallied forth from their red-roofed barracks on long and gruelling patrols. With an Indian guide breaking trail on snowshoes, they would lope behind their dog-teams, urging on slant-eyed huskies with snapping lash, the frigid air ringing with the merry tinkle of sleigh-bells. As night descended, and trees burst asunder with biting frost, they would dig a hole in the snow-drifts, build a roaring campfire, thaw out grub and dog-feed and crawl, shivering, into their eiderdown robes. At all times keeping a vigilant watch over trapper, trader, redman and Eskimo alike. Not, however, till 1928 was well under way did C. H. "Punch" Dickins of Western Canada Airways commence seriously to blaze new trails into the heart of this region.

On March 6th Dickins crossed the Arctic Circle and, on July 1st, set down his pontoon-equipped Fokker before a crowd of admiring traders, trappers and Eskimos at Aklavic, Arctic "metropolis," only sixty miles from the Polar Sea. By this time this new form of aerial transportation, at first frowned upon by old-timers, had already caught public favour as a welcome escape from the drudgery and hardships of dog-team and canoe travel. For not only did it prove immeasurably faster but less expensive in the long run.

When I found myself at Fort Resolution that spring, making my usual round of Great Slave Lake by dog-team, Doctor Bourget, the Indian Agent, told me he proposed to fly with "Punch" Dickins to Fort Providence and back the following day. An hour after leaving the fort next morning we heard "Punch" revving up his machine and within a few minutes his Fokker went sailing by overhead, to disappear to the northward. A couple of hours later, after we had covered a scant twelve miles by dog-team, my driver, John James Daniels, pointed ahead.

"Look, *Okemow*," he grunted, "noder plane!"

But it was *not* another plane. It was only "Punch" returning to Fort

Resolution, having flown to Fort Providence and back, some two hundred-odd miles. At that moment the realization was driven home to me that dog-team travel was already on its way out.

It was later that Dickins made his remarkable 1,540 mile flight from Edmonton to Aklavic in the short space of seventeen-hours flying time, giving the local Nunatagmuits the thrill of their lives. Hardly had he landed when these friendly children of the Polar spaces were about him on all sides, clamouring for rides. One ancient beldame alone was skeptical. "I don't believe it," she insisted. "It couldn't fly. Its wings won't flap!"

To which a grinning Huskie countered: "It looks like a bird all right, but I doubt if there's much meat on it!"

While "Punch" was piling up new records through the summer of 1929 his associate, Leigh Brintnell of Winnipeg, was not idle. Taking off from Lac du Bonnett in August with Gilbert Labine aboard, he hopped to Fort McMurray via The Pas, thence down the Mackenzie to Fort Norman; picked up Bill Boland, former Hudson's Bay factor at Fort Good Hope, and flew them into Great Bear Lake. From there he headed to Aklavic, took aboard more passengers and, in less than seven hours, had completed the first flight from there to Dawson City. Next day he headed south along the Pacific Coast, across country to Edmonton, The Pas and Winnipeg, little realizing the far-reaching effect that flight to lonely Great Bear Lake was to have in the future opening-up and mining development of that forgotten land.

Meanwhile, "Wop" May's experiences had proven no exception to those of so many other pilots who found themselves facing frustration in seeking to rehabilitate themselves whilst clinging to an overpowering desire to dedicate themselves to the cause of Aviation. The May Aeroplanes, organized by him and Court in 1919, had been

Note: The startling changes in transportation introduced by the aeroplane can be fully appreciated by comparing the author's dog-team journey in January 1924 from Aklavic to Fairbanks with Leigh Brintnell's seven hour 'plane journey from Great Bear Lake to Dawson City Y.T. in 1929.

Leaving Aklavic by dog-team on January 2nd, 1924, it took the writer 17 days' arduous travel to reach Fort Yukon; 4 additional days from there to Circle City and an additional 10 days through blizzards and heavy snow to Fairbanks, Alaska; 31 days in all compared with less than 7 hours by Leigh Brintnell's plane only five years later.—P.H.G.

foredoomed to failure since the public had yet to be educated into becoming air-minded, and because there was a total absence of any close and active mining development in the Northwest which would create a demand for airborne freight or passenger service.

While suffering a temporary setback, Captain May's mind was still in the skies. The necessity for earning a living had forced him into accepting employment in a totally different sphere, as had been the case with Walter Gilbert and countless others. But the confinement irked his soul and he longed for the excitement and adventure to which he had grown accustomed, and which only his first love—flying—could provide. In close touch with aviation developments, and the resurgence of flying in the mining areas of Ontario, he turned his face again towards the North. Meeting a kindred soul in the person of Vic Horner of Edmonton, they pooled part of their resources in a small Avro Avian plane with which to pit their courage and experience against the gods of chance.

6

MERCY FLIGHT TO FORT VERMILION

New Year's Day, 1929, had been ushered into the frontier town of Peace River Crossing on the heels of Keewatin—God of the North Wind. A howling blizzard roared down from the Pole, its stinging clouds of swirling snow obliterating the pines and cottonwoods, and Twelve Foot Davis's lofty grave atop the steep pinnacle of *Esputinaw* which lifted its bulk into the frigid skies. Long since, half-breeds and trappers had hauled out their moccasins and fringed buckskin *capotes*, while the Mounted Police had jettisoned scarlet serges for short buffalo coats, otterskin caps and moose-skin mittens. In from the woods, trappers were engaged in a round of alcoholic joviality, momentarily forgetting the trials of the trapline, whilst *Métis* and Cree braves celebrated *O-chay-may-keesikow*, or Kissing Day, by osculatory assaults on all the coy maidens they could gather in their dusky arms. Over in the dance hall a cosmopolitan gathering of mixed Northerners—Indians, half-breeds and squaws—were pounding their way through the intricacies of the *Red River Jig* and *Eightsome Reel* to the thump! thump! of moccasined feet and the mingled strains of tom-toms and squeaking fiddles.

In the distance the silvery tinkle of sleigh-bells echoed through the snow-laden evergreens. Out of the bush to the eastward emerged an Indian runner, the hood of his frost-rimed *capote* pulled about his face as he bent his cowled head into the biting wind, his curved snowshoes kicking up clouds of powdery snow.

"Marche! Marche!" The hoarse voice of Louis Bourassa, mail-carrier from Fort Vermilion, twelve days down-river, urged his tired sleigh-dogs in the snowshoe trail tramped down by his Indian foregoer. Small knots of revellers, emerging momentarily from the warmth of hotel and cabin, wondered why the dogs looked worn and played-out, and why Louis, instead of making for the hilarity of the Peace Hotel, had headed his huskies up the old Lesser Slave Lake trail. Halting his dog-team before the telegraph office, Louis lunged through the door and, drawing a telegram from within his smoked moose-skin *capote*, handed it to Pierre Gauvereau, the operator.

The facetious welcome on the tip of Pierre's tongue died when he observed the worn, lined visage framed in the frosted hood of the *coureur.* Then, as his eyes ran over the telegram, his face turned grave and there was an urgency to his finger as he rattled the metal key to send the cry for aid from the stricken settlement of Fort Vermilion to Edmonton.

Darkness had fallen when the message reached Dr. M. R. Bow, Deputy Minister of Health for Alberta. Signed by H. A. Hamman, Indian Doctor, it read:

Logan, Hudson's Bay man at Red River fifty miles below Fort Vermilion bad case of diphtheria. Voice gone and throat para- lyzed. Serum old. Have started immunizing people around, but quantity limited. Several known contacts five to nine days ago. If possible rush aeroplane. Good landing and no snow. If snow, will clear landing strip at both Fort Vermilion and Red River. Radio message to me when to expect plane. Send intubation apparatus and several hundred units antitoxin toxoid for two hundred people. Cannot leave Logan's bedside. Real emergency. Do all possible.

A post-script to the original wire added that Bert Logan had died shortly after it was written!

The message, Dr. Bow noted with concern, was dated December 18th, and had been wired from Peace River on January 1st. That meant that the dog-driver had been on the trail for two weeks, fighting his way through bitter cold, deep snow and blinding blizzards to carry the wire to the nearest telegraph office.

Realizing the virulence of such an epidemic, and the susceptibility of the Indians and *Métis* who comprised the major portion of the population of three or four hundred souls, it was hard to say to what extent the isolated and helpless settlement, six hundred long miles to the northward, had been ravaged during those twelve days.

In the bitter weather that had taken possession of the North it seemed out of the question to expect anyone to attempt to make the trip in an open-cockpit plane. Yet, at least two weeks must elapse if the life-saving antitoxin was forwarded by train to Peace River, and thence by the return of Louis Bourassa's dog-team to Fort Vermilion. By that time the epidemic could easily be stalking the Indian camps throughout the whole length of the lower Peace River and adjacent country, carrying death in its train. There was, of course, "Wop" May. But, could even "Wop," hardened and resourceful flyer that he was, be expected to gamble his life in a flight over unknown territory in such bitter and devastating cold? Even as the doctor turned this over in his mind a frigid blast shook the house, and driving snow pelted remorselessly against the frosted window panes.

Picking up the telephone he dialled "Wop's" number. "I hate to disturb you," the doctor apologized, "but it's a case of life or death. Fort Vermilion's down with a diphtheria epidemic of the most virulent kind. Bert Logan died on December 18th, the day the dog-runner headed for Peace River with the message I have just received from Dr. Hamman. He says a supply of antitoxin's imperative. Wants it by plane!"

"Wop's" reply was characteristically curt and concise. "Get your antitoxin lined up. Vic Horner and I'll hit the trail for Fort Vermilion in the morning." The phone clicked off.

Next day the *Edmonton Bulletin*, which always kept a friendly eye on "Wop," and insisted upon looking on him as a native son, announced the prospective mercy flight in red headlines accompanied by flowery and somewhat imaginative prose:

TREMENDOUS ODDS FACING
PLANE IN NORTHERN FLIGHT

Race against Death by "Wop" May and Vic Horner in tiny Avian will go down in history as gallant effort.

A country ravaged by a dragon! A knight in shining armour riding forth to slay the dragon. Six hundred miles to the north of Edmonton, beyond the reach of telegraph, the dread dragon of diphtheria has stalked through the land for more than two weeks now.

Only one doctor and close to three hundred miles of wilderness between them and the nearest telegraph office. A crack musher, before him a panting team of huskies, half-hiding their driver in the fog of steam from their frozen breaths, comes through with a cry for aid after twelve gruelling days on the winter trail! "One white man is dead; others have caught the disease. Rush antitoxin!"

Over the humming wires the message sped to the Department of Health in Edmonton. Antitoxin and toxoid were gathered and then—

Two knights of the skies, throwing their lives in a desperate hazard with death, riding a slender and fragile thing of wood and silk and steel; their steed a shining plane; their weapon a whirling propeller which lops off the cold, white miles, one by one.

And these two knights of the skies are risking their lives to save the lives of others—behind them in their plane ride gleaming glass tubes carrying the hope of life—600,000 units of diphtheria antitoxin and enough toxoid to handle close to two hundred and fifty cases . . .

Before the flyers is space, the illimitable skies; behind them doubts and fears. Not for the ability of the flyers but for their chance of survival in a light machine in mid-winter heading into an unknown wilderness with the ultimate risk of landing on rough ice, or making a forced landing on some nameless lake in unknown terrain with wheels.

But to "Wop" and his partner it was all just part of a day's work as he and Vic climbed into the fore and aft cockpits of the 75-horse-power machine, with the precious package of antitoxin handed them by Dr. Bow carefully tucked away in rugs, with charcoal heaters to keep it from freezing, gave the little Avian the gun and soared into the murky sky.

Between Edmonton and Peace River lay three hundred and twenty miles of muskeg and matted spruce which, for years, had served as a barrier to the white invasion of the Peace River country; a forested wilderness pierced only by the runways of animals, a few bush trails,

Mercy flight from Edmonton to Fort Vermilion, Alberta, January 2, 1929. Left to right: Ambrose Upton Gledstanes Bury, mayor of Edmonton; Vic Horner; "Wop" May; Dr. M.R. Bow, Deputy Minister of Health.
Glenbow Archives NA-1821-2

and the meandering steel ribbons of the Edmonton-Dunvegan and British Columbia Railway, where, even in mid-summer, frost lurked within a few inches of the surface and which seemed, in winter, to attract both heavy snow and intense cold.

Despite their heavy clothing it did not take long for the biting headwind and bitter cold to penetrate to the very marrow and soon both fliers were almost petrified. To add to their difficulties, an overcast sky loaded with swirling snow reduced visibility at times to nil, while it was necessary to fly so low as to almost skim the jagged spruce-tops that rose into the murky heavens like the spears of an avenging army.

The judgment of railroads in selecting townsites isn't always to be commended, and this certainly applied to the E.D. & B.C. Railway in sacrificing the picturesqueness of Grouard Settlement, overlooking Buffalo Bay on Lesser Slave Lake, for the crude and dingy divisional point of McLennan in the heart of a muskeg—dotted with scrub spruce.

Grey skies were giving place to purple, shot with fiery arcs of sunset, when the frozen fliers, circling the little railroad town, beheld with a surge of relief a primitive landing field, marked out on the ice of nearby Round Lake in twin lines of lopped-off spruce trees, which had been cleared and prepared for their possible need by Leon Giroux and a force of townspeople.

Draining the oil from the engine, the fliers made their way to the hotel under the acclaim of those who had swarmed down to the landing field to meet them.

Bright and early next morning they were up, Vic Horner warming up the oil over a fire kindled near the plane, while "Wop," heedless of carbon monoxide fumes, sucked out the engine ere warming it up with a blow-torch under a home-made hangar devised from a tattered tarpaulin that heaved and swayed with the wind that had arisen to bedevil them.

By ten-thirty they were high over the mighty Peace River, now frozen to marble immobility in the grasp of the Frost King. Beneath them lay a magnificent panorama of rolling hills and snow-blanketed prairie through which, like a huge ribbon of silver, meandered the

77

stately Peace—joined a few miles to the westward by the sombre Smoky as it emerged from its purple-shadowed canyon. *Sagitawa*, The Meeting of the Waters, the Crees called it. Upon the topmost pinnacle of a steep hill overlooking the diminutive town of Peace River Crossing flashed a white dot, the headstone marking the resting place of Twelve Foot Davis upon which "Peace River Jim" Cornwall had inscribed the words: "He was every man's friend and never locked his cabin door."

A hurriedly-cleared landing-place on the usually rough ice of the river below the bank again made it possible for the fliers to make a landing with their wheels without experiencing any trouble. Taking only time enough to refuel the plane and get thawed out, they prepared to tackle the last 280 miles of the flight to Fort Vermilion, where a crack dog-team waited to carry the antitoxin fifty miles to the other stricken settlement at Red River.

"We don't expect to have any trouble landing with wheels at Fort Vermilion," "Wop" told Mr. Levesque and the rest of the Peace Riverites who, with blue noses and constant application of hands to frozen ears, crowded down to the ice to see them off. "Dr. Bow's been radioing Fort Vermilion that we're coming. We figure on finding a landing place ready for us on Sheridan Lawrence's ranch across the river."

A moment later and the diminutive Avian was on its way. Until it returned to Peace River its movements, and the success, or otherwise, of the flight, would be a secret known only to the wilderness into which it was embarking.

As the two men were swallowed up in the Unknown a twinge of conscience seemed to afflict some of the newspapers to the southward. One daily editorialized:

With the lives of five hundred persons at a wilderness post at stake the Government of Alberta should not gamble everything on the audacious courage of two Edmonton fliers and the air-worthiness of a tiny Avian plane. A second plane should have been dispatched at once to act as a reserve to that now supposedly winging its way over the uninhabited stretch of country lying between Peace River and Fort Vermilion. In other parts of Canada where rescue and relief planes have been sent into isolated country, two planes have been used. It is far below zero weather in the North today, and the plane used by Captain May and Vic Horner has no enclosed cabin. The threat of snow adds to the difficulties of flight over the wilderness. If the plane is forced down in the wilderness it will be days or even weeks before news can reach the Outside. Even if the fliers reach Fort Vermilion today, Edmonton cannot know it for nearly two weeks and in the meantime the authorities' hands are tied by ignorance of what has happened. The provincial government deserves every credit for what it has already done, but if anything should happen to May and Horner the people of Alberta will hold the government to blame for a blot on the escutcheon of the province caused by a willingness to gamble with human lives instead of incurring the expense required to lessen the hazards on this flight of mercy.

As the short, cold winter days slipped by, a feeling of anxiety hovered over the Northwest. The imagination and daring of the flight had taken possession of the country to such an extent that the safety of the fliers outweighed the plight of the marooned people of the northern settlements in their grim fight with the epidemic until, with a vast number, it became a personal thing.

As the sun dropped behind the sombre escarpment guarding the ice-girded Smoky on January 5th, suffusing the purple-shadowed sky with lemon and scarlet, John McElroy stepped from his home on the fringe of Peace River town and searched the eastern sky for perhaps the twentieth time that day. The roar of an aeroplane engine was wafted to his ears. There was no mistake about it! Pulling the hood of his *parka* over his head, he tore down the lane to carry the news. Others, including a couple of Mounted Policemen who had heard the welcome sound, were rushing pell-mell to the river ice. Then, as quietly and unostentatiously as it had taken off, the sturdy little Avian darted out of the skies and settled on the snow.

Prematurely aged and lined by the strain and exposure, there was a grey, mask-like caricature of a grin on the faces of both "Wop" May and Vic Horner as the two half-frozen but stout-hearted men had to be physically lifted from the open cockpits by willing helpers, "Wop's" hands having to be literally pried loose from the controls. In no time they were whipped into a waiting car and whisked off over the Hart River and along the road paralleling the frozen Peace to the red-roofed barracks of the Royal Canadian Mounted Police. Under the kindly ministrations of the police, the two men were quickly transformed from veritable icicles into warm and appreciative humans, their trail-frozen *parkas* exchanged for dry, clean clothing, and the inner man fortified against the cold.

Around the panting, red-hot stove at the barracks the fliers spoke in warmest tones of the splendid reception given them by Gus Clarke of the Hudson's Bay Company, Dr. Hamman and the people to whom they had carried the life-saving serum. Travelling through the biting cold on the last long hop in the open cockpits had, they admitted, been an endurance test, while, on their arrival at Fort Vermilion, both were so stiff and frozen they had to be lifted from the plane. No difficulties had been encountered apart from the return trip when, owing to the poor quality of the gas obtained at the Fort, the engine had frequently threatened to conk out and leave them to make the best of a perilous landing on the hummocky river ice, with the prospect of hoofing it a hundred-odd miles on snowshoes. Fortunately, on each occasion, it had picked up, but not before both had experienced some decidedly unpleasant qualms, the erratic behaviour of the engine leaving them with a haunting sense of insecurity and uneasiness throughout the flight.

As soon as the tiny Avian plane soared into the sky from the icy runway at Peace River on the last lap of the homeward flight at noon next day the news was flashed to Edmonton over the swaying telegraph wires by Pierre Gauvereau. Long before they could possibly arrive in Edmonton a procession of cars, trucks and pedestrians swept towards the airport. From all directions, the welcoming avalanche poured into the air-field until thousands bucked the bitter cold to meet the returning fliers.

Meanwhile, G. C. Becker, President of the Edmonton and Northern

Alberta Flying Club, took off with M. Brinkman, the club's mechanic, in a Moth plane to intercept the returning argonauts and escort them in. But a renewal of blizzard-like conditions forced a hasty return.

Suddenly there appeared from out of the soft falling snow the tiny Avian a scant hundred feet above the ground. To the surprise of the two aviators, they found the landing field crowded by a cheering, howling throng of thousands. For a moment "Wop" couldn't make sure whether the cheers signified relief that the people at Fort Vermilion had been saved or that he and Vic had returned safely since, to "Wop," it was just another good job done—all part of the day's work.

Almost before anyone was aware of it, "Wop" had made a landing safely beside the hangar, to be surrounded by a cheering throng. As he hauled himself from the cockpit he appeared to be about all-in, but Vic hopped out, fresh and smiling, looking none the worse for the trip. Next moment the two startled aviators were seized by the crowd, hoisted shoulder-high and carried in triumph to the hangar. Here, an impromptu ceremony took place. His Worship, Mayor A. U. G. Bury, stepped forward and officially welcomed the fliers home. Later, on behalf of a group of twenty leading businessmen, illuminated addresses and gold watches were presented to the two men in appreciation of their epochal flight.

To inquiring reporters, Captain May, enigmatic and sparing of words as usual, insisted that the entire trip had proven uneventful so far as excitement was concerned. Everything had succeeded according to plan, he stated. The greatest difficulty encountered was with the engine—due both to cold and the poor gasoline with which they had refueled the engine at Fort Vermilion. When they refilled at the fort there was available only a total quantity of fifteen gallons of gas. It was providential for them, "Wop" added, that this was there as, only by chance, had Dr. Hamman brought it back from Little Red River. After leaving Peace River on the return trip, blinding snow reduced visibility to such an extent that most of the trip was completed at an altitude of about a hundred-feet.

The *Western Tribune* of Vancouver, under dateline of January 12th, paid a fitting tribute to this outstanding mercy flight:

Canadians were thrilled last week to read of the heroic exploit of Captain Wilfred May and Lieutenant Victor Horner, both of Edmonton, in flying 650 miles through bitterly cold winds to Fort Vermilion and Little Red River in order to provide antitoxin that was sorely needed because of diphtheria epidemic.

The feat, which was nothing more or less than a sublime gamble with death, on an errand of unalloyed mercy, must forever be associated with the great deeds of men since time began. It rivals the heroism of Balaclava and Lucknow. If anything, it outshines them.

Had the tiny Avian plane foundered in its flight; had the dauntless aviators met death in the lonely northern wilds, their names would have been enshrined in the hearts of men, women and children all over the world. But the machine got through. As a consequence, it is probable that little has been heard about this exploit outside of the Dominion. And even Canadians will be apt to forget as time goes unless something is done to perpetuate the story of this magnificent exploit.

Thus was established the pattern for many future mercy flights that were, in time, to become almost commonplace episodes in Northern life, and also the inspiration for the Air Rescue School which "Wop" was to establish years later for the R.C.A.F.'s Western and Northwestern Commands with its teams of efficiently-trained "Parasearchers."

Shortly after their return, "Wop" and Vic left Edmonton, ostensibly for a holiday trip to get away from the round of entertainment that had since pursued them. Actually, the two fliers left for Los Angeles, headquarters for the Lockheed Aircraft Corporation, to purchase a plane similar to the type Sir Hubert Wilkins had used so successfully on his Antarctic expedition. The *Edmonton Bulletin* wrote:

While details of the Lockheed "Vega" plane are not yet fully known it is said that it is the fastest commercial plane made, and can fly with a heavy load of passengers. Denials were given by

"Wop" and Vic before leaving here that they were going to invest more heavily still in the air transport business, but it is thought that the plane will be used for making trips into the northland in competition with the Fokker now flying in there for the Western Canada Airways. The Lockheed "Vega" will be "ship" number two of the Commercial Airways, the first unit being the Avian in which "Wop" and Vic made their flight to Fort Vermilion. Cy Becker, well-known flier, is a partner in the concern along with the other two fliers.

Despite these denials, "Wop" arrived back in Edmonton on Sunday, February 10th, bringing back from its Burbank factory the Lockheed "Vega" monoplane after completing a 2,100 mile flight.

While "Wop" was establishing new aerial conquests in more mercy flights into the heart of the unfolding Peace River country, "Punch" Dickins was engaging in a different but equally exacting type of aerial pioneering, laying the foundations for future air mail routes from Fort McMurray, at the end-of-steel, to Fort Simpson in the heart of the Northwest Territories.

Ever since Walter Hale—"The Flying Postmaster," as he was to be known—made his first exploratory trip by scow and sternwheeler into the North in the fall of 1921 he had been impressed with the immensity of the Northwest Territories and the need for improving the postal service from the primitive dog-team, with its obvious limitations, to something more in keeping with this modern age. By 1924 the potentialities of an aerial mail service had already caught Walter's active imagination and, as a result, C.H. "Punch" Dickins, then a flying officer with the R.C.A.F., submitted a report which proved to be uncannily correct in its prediction regarding the value of the plane for wilderness communication.

It was not until Friday, January 18th, 1929, that "Punch" was able to put his theories into effect and undertake an experimental mail flight. Accompanied by Post Office Inspector T. J. Reilly of Edmonton, and air-engineer Lew Parmenter, he soared into the frigid skies in a cabined Fokker Super-Universal, G-CASN, and headed for Fort Simpson.

But the day proved unpropitious. Only forty miles out, they were forced to limp back to Edmonton as a result of the biting cold causing ice particles to plug the carburetor. Not until the 23rd did the Fokker hop from Lac la Biche to Fort McMurray and head for the north in a chilling temperature of 58° below zero. At Fort Smith receding water had created ice-hummocks of such proportions that the aircraft landed in a series of breath-taking bumps and bounces reminiscent of Captain Gorman's disastrous experience on the Mission field at Fort Simpson years before. Battling bitter 62° below weather and execrable landing places, "Punch" succeeded in delivering his mail at Fort Chipewyan, Fort Smith, Fort Resolution, Hay River and, finally at Fort Simpson where, taking aboard that famed and colourful fur trader, "Rags" Wilson, as passenger, he headed back towards the dismal aloofness of Fort Resolution.

As they swooped down from the frost-misted skies to an improvised landing field on the bleak ice of Great Slave Lake there was a grinding crash as the undercarriage struck a snow-drifted ice-hummock. Down dipped the nose until the tip of the all-metal propeller was curled into a graceful scroll and the other seriously bent.

With the characteristic resourcefulness that has been the hallmark of Canada's pioneer bush pilots and their mechanics, Dickins and Lew started to work on the cold, wind-swept waterfront. The front of the plane was jacked onto gas barrels while the shattered undercarriage was roughly mended with a water-pipe furnished by the Roman Catholic Mission. Next, came the heart-breaking task of straightening the metal blades in a forty-below temperature, in the face of a wicked wind whining across the endless miles of ice, and inadequate tools for the purpose. One aluminum blade was straightened out, but while working on the twisted prop nine priceless inches of aluminum snapped off. Again it seemed as though, like their predecessor, Gorman, they were fated to remain marooned in that lonely spot, six hundred miles from civilization, or be forced to resort to the much-maligned and despised dog-team, thus spelling the doom of the air mail for years to come!

Faced by this last disaster, Dickins hired a Slavey Indian to set out with his dog-team to carry a message to Fort Smith, six "sleeps" to the southward, for transmission to Edmonton, ordering repair parts.

"Supposing," "Punch" asked Lew next morning, "we let the one prop go as it is, and file nine inches off the other blade—do you think the ruddy plane would fly?"

Lew's answer was to dive into his fur *parka* and grab his mitts. Next day the aircraft was ready for the test. "Punch" taxied up and down the treacherous ice of Resolution Bay then, giving her the gun, soared gently into the air. The old crate would fly after all! That night they landed safely at Fort Smith with their attenuated propeller, and headed south for home.

That fall the heroic work of the little Avian and the Lockheed Vega, now known as Commercial Airways, sparked still another colourful enterprise, linking it with the Routledge Air Service of Calgary, and involving an outlay of $100,000.00 for a further assault upon the Frozen Frontier in establishing a Government-sponsored air mail service from Edmonton to the rim of the Polar Sea—the outcome of "Punch" Dickins' successful mail-test flight the previous January.

While "Wop" May, and George Hoskins of the Routledge Company, headed for Eastern Canada to fly back three big Bellanca cabin-monoplanes to add to the Lockheed Vega in this new conquest of the Northern wastes, Harvey Mills of the combined companies gave his story to the press. "At present," he told reporters, "winter travel from Fort McMurray to Aklavic by dog-team occupies two months, under the very best conditions. The Northland is virtually closed to the Outside world for eight months of the year. This new mail project will serve Fort Smith, Fort Norman and all other trading posts along the Mackenzie River to the delta at Aklavic. The main trip to this settlement, a distance of 1,500 air miles, will be accomplished in less than twenty hours' flying time, the return journey occupying *four days* as compared with *four months* in the past!"

7

LOST PLANES AND LOST MEN

The summer of 1929 became an historic year in Canada's great hinterland. The whole world was speculation mad, and capital could be secured from the money barons of the East for almost any enterprise. A Toronto promoter, asking for five million dollars for aerial exploration and prospecting in the North, amassed it almost overnight. The two "Thunder Birds" that had invaded the fastnesses of the North eight years before had hatched a mighty brood whose drone-like humming now filled the northern skies. No longer did Hornby's Barrens offer insuperable obstacles to transportation. Prospecting parties shuttled backwards and forwards in their aerial taxis in a minimum of time and with a maximum of comfort.

On September 8th, Colonel C. D. H. MacAlpine of the Dominion Explorers, and a party consisting of Alex Milne and Dick Pearce, editor of the *Northern Miner*, set out from The Pas in two planes—a Fokker and a Fairchild—piloted by "Tommy" Thompson and Stan McMillan, for Baker Lake in the barren tundra north-west of Fort Churchill en route to the copper deposits of the Coppermine, intending to fly to Aklavic by way of Bathurst Inlet, Great Bear Lake and Fort Norman.

While the Colonel had already made a couple of trips north there was one important feature the party had overlooked, and that was the fierce equinoctial storms that sweep with such devastating fury across the open tundra and the Arctic coastal barrier around this time of the year. Furthermore, the Barrens were not prepared to surrender their ancient sway without a fight. In an unguarded moment they had permitted one or two parties to fly across their dreary width but now, with all the vigour and impetuosity of old, they prepared to crack down on these puny humans as they had on Samuel Hearne, the first white man to dare their ancient terrors in an attempt to reach the Coppermine. Hearne's historic attack on the isolation of the Barrens had occurred exactly one-hundred-and-sixty years before, and has been preserved for posterity in his interesting *Journal*. Goaded into activity by accusations that they were failing to fulfill the obligations of their Royal Charter and explore the interior, the Hudson's Bay Company commissioned Samuel Hearne, Captain of the brig

Charlotte, to proceed overland from Fort Churchill to the "Far-off-Metal-River"—the Coppermine—of which reports had reached the Company from wandering Indians, and which was now the object of the MacAlpine search.

At daybreak on November 6th, 1769, the occupants of Fort Prince of Wales—whose massive ruins still dominate Churchill Harbour—assembled in the bitter cold to witness the explorer's departure. A salute of seven guns and ringing cheers was responded to by Hearne with a wave of his cap and he was swallowed up in the salty mist that rolled inland from the Bay. On December 11th he reeled back into the fort, defeated by a combination of atrocious weather and the desertion of his Indian guides. On February 23rd, 1770, he set out once again, only to be driven back by adverse circumstances, starvation and exposure. Twice baffled, he departed once more on December 7th, 1770, this time accompanied by the redoubtable Chipewyan guide, Mattonabee, and, on July 14th, 1771, nearly two years after his original departure, gazed over the dancing surface of the Coppermine. Descending the stream to its mouth, he beheld the Arctic Ocean—the first white man to reach the Polar Sea overland! It was a story of incredible hardship, suffering and privation, in which the Barrens displayed their fickleness and terror in all their frustrating phases.

It was not, however, necessary to go this far back to realize the pitiful inadequacy of attempting to conquer the Barrens by time-worn snowshoes and dog-team. One has only to recall the five years' search of Inspector Beyts and Inspector Frank French of the North West Mounted Police for the Eskimo killers of Radford and Street, on the shores of Bathurst Inlet, which led them over the identical route that the MacAlpine Expedition expected to fly in a matter of hours. Menaced by hordes of ravening wolves; snaring Arctic hares or ptarmigan to eke out diminishing rations; lacking always the friendly comfort of a campfire, Beyts and his men pushed into the heart of the frozen Barrens, engaged in the gruelling task of killing caribou and setting up meat caches between Baker Lake and the Thelon to provide dog-feed for the forthcoming trip to Bathurst Inlet. Twice thrown back on his base at Chesterfield Inlet by pitiless and unrelenting cold and a shortage of dog-feed, Beyts, physically broken by an over-whelming succession of crushing blows and hardships, was replaced by the athletic Frank French.

On March 21st, 1917, Inspector French and Sergeant-Major Caulkin made still another assault on the invincible Barrens that, since the dawn of time, had resisted all man's efforts to conquer them. Again it was a story of galling hardships, starvation and bitter cold; of famished dogs, eluding the vigilance of their masters, devouring their harness, or turning cannibal and rending each other apart; of an unheard of assault upon their camp by famished wolves. For an hour men and dogs fought the attacking grey squadrons until the beasts withdrew in sullen fury to devour their dead and lick their wounds.

By December 22nd their plight was desperate. Sleds and baggage had been abandoned as dogs died of starvation. Out of food, desper-ate, and still four hundred miles from their destination, French's drooping eyes caught a glimpse of curved imprints on the blue drifts at his feet. The tracks of musk-oxen! That day twenty of these massive animals fell before the bullets of their Eskimo guide, Bye-Bye. Yet, on January 11th, 1918, they were wrestling again with that bugbear of the Barrens—starvation!

"Bitch Ticktack had seven pups," French wrote in his *Journal*. "Killed some and fed them to the dogs . . ."

Times had changed—but *not* the Barrens—these modern adventur-ers were soon to learn! On the evening of their departure, Pilot "Tommy" Thompson radioed the following message:—

"Arrived Baker Lake. Leaving in morning for Bathurst Inlet."

From that moment on, the MacAlpine party disappeared com-pletely from human ken. Before leaving, they had let it be known that they expected to arrive at Fort Norman on September 23rd, but, for some inexplicable reason, had insisted that—in event of being over-due—no search was to be made for them until the lapse of at least ten days!

When days sped by, with the Arctic maintaining an inexorable silence regarding their fate, anxiety spread apace. In this "in-between" season landing conditions on the Northern lakes would be precarious in the extreme, especially for planes equipped, as were those of the MacAlpine party, with only pontoons, and many of the smaller lakes would already be covered with a fragile skin of thin ice which would make landing with either pontoons or skis impossible. Further concern was given by a faint message from the Hudson's Bay Company's post at Bathurst Inlet to the effect that the expedition had failed to pass that point. The only inference was that the party had met with some serious mishap between Baker Lake and Bathurst.

As newspapers flashed flaming headlines across their front pages concerning "THE LOST MacALPINE PARTY," General D. M. Hogarth with a party of five arrived in Winnipeg from Toronto and, after establishing headquarters in the Grain Exchange Building, proceeded to organize what was to prove the greatest flying search in the history of Canadian aviation.

Fifteen of the best-known and most experienced pilots, nearly all of whom had received their initial training the hard way in the skies of France, participated in the search, while Western Canada Airways, the Dominion Explorers and Consolidated Smelters pooled both planes and resources to comb the Barrens for the missing men.

With Andy Cruickshank directing activities, the first planes that headed into the North in this momentous search were two super-Fokkers, belonging to Western Canada Airways, piloted by H. Hollick-Kenyon and Roy F. Brown. These were quickly followed by two Dominion Explorers planes, with Charlie Sutton and Jimmie Spence at the controls.

The fact that the Expedition had failed to reach Bernard Harbour led to the conclusion that the planes were down somewhere in the barren lake-bejewelled moors between there and Baker Lake. Since all were experienced in northern conditions, and well-equipped with emergency rations and winter clothing, there was a good chance they would still be alive, though living conditions in the open, treeless tundra would be far more exacting than a forced landing in the bush—where a warming fire and shelter was merely a matter of using axes. On the tundra there would be little or no shelter other than what could be derived from piling up rock-walls, while the only fire obtainable would be from half-green willows and dried moss. The general impression was that the planes had been frozen, and anchored, on some small lake, unable to take off.

Acting on this theory, Roy Brown and Jimmie Spence headed for Athabasca Lake and made an epic flight across the Barren Lands from Stony Rapids to Baker Lake without result, while "Punch" Dickins made an equally momentous flight from Fort Smith to the mouth of the Coppermine and back between September 28th and 30th, following this by a further long flight to Fort Reliance, down the Back's River to Bathurst Inlet and along the turbulent Thelon through Hornby's stamping grounds, back to the capital of the Northwest Territories.

Next, Roy Brown and Jimmie Spence headed for the cache at Beverley Lake. Examining it, they discovered evidence of a recent visit together with the fact that the supplies were gone. Roy gazed speculatively over the stark and utter desolation by which they were surrounded. In all directions—north, south, east and west—extended the grey-white reaches of the Land that God Forgot beneath a cold and threatening sky. Not a stick, not a tree, not even a solitary hill were there to break the dread monotony or give perspective. No shadows, not a thing with which the eye could measure distance! Like the dirge of lost souls, the wind moaned dolefully by in the same deadly, unending refrain until it nearly drove one mad. The utter immensity of this vast, illimitable No-Man's-Land, inhabited only by the migratory caribou, the Arctic hare, the sharp-eyed white fox and the gaunt wolf, dulled one's very soul and stultified the imagination. It was like a world of nothingness enveloped with a winding-sheet of snow.

"Looks like they left here some time ago," Roy mused. "Probably hit for the coast and got marooned there after they ran out of gas!"

"And, if we don't hit back to the base," Spence admitted grudgingly, "we'll be in the same damn boat ourselves."

Despite gas shortage, they flew on to Pelly Lake—to be faced again with disappointment and frustration.

Meanwhile, I.W. Soloway and Harvey Mills had proffered the help of Commercial Airways, and hardly had "Wop" May landed at Cooking Lake on October 3rd with the new Bellanca, after a four-day flight from Montreal, than a report that "Punch" Dickins was missing in the Barrens sent him hurtling north to participate in the search. At the same time, "Con" Farrell, together with other experienced Western Canada Airways pilots stationed at The Pas, continued to relay gas and other supplies to Stony Rapids, at the east end of Athabasca Lake, and across the tundra to Clinton-Colden Lake and other appointed caches.

Fear for the safety of the lost fliers was growing. While the MacAlpine Expedition had been well supplied with winter clothing, rations, ammunition and fishing tackle, winter might crack down at any moment with all its Arctic severity. Furthermore, ice was already forming on the larger lakes, yet conditions were such that it would still be impossible for the rescue planes to take off on skis. In desperation, Andy Cruickshank and Hollick-Kenyon decided on a last-chance dash across the Barrens on a seven-hundred mile flight to Stony Rapids and Baker Lake. Then, like a thunderbolt, on November 4th came the faint message from Ross Smythe, youthful McGill University student and "Sparks" aboard the Hudson's Bay Company's S. S. *Fort James* at Gjoa Haven on King William's Land, graveyard of the Franklin Expedition: "MacAlpine and party found. All well. Located Cambridge Bay."[1]

Toying with his radio aboard the snow-bound vessel, he had received the faint but startling words from Ian McKinnon, a Hudson's Bay Company's clerk, who had managed to transmit it from the *Bay Maud*, in winter quarters at Cambridge Bay.

A couple of days later, Captain G. S. Blanchet, veteran northern surveyor and explorer who had joined the rescue party at Great Slave Lake, radioed from Bathurst Inlet that three of the rescue planes were headed for the Hudson's Bay Company's post at Cambridge Bay to pick up the MacAlpine party, but had been forced down by adverse weather.

Early next morning, Guy Blanchet, in company with Hollick-Kenyon, Roy Brown and Jimmie Spence, headed across ice-filled

1. This post was established by the author in 1923 when making an official inspection of the Western Arctic District for the Hudson's Bay Company. Another post, Fort Brabant—now Fort Collinson—was established by the writer near the foot of Prince Albert Sound on Victoria Island the same summer.—P.H.G.

Dease Straits, picked up the entire party, and returned to the Canalaska post at Burnside River just as dusk was falling. However, though the party had been located and flown over to the mainland along with the genial Major Lockie Burwash, they were still not out of the Barrens which, with characteristic treachery, now proceeded to again crack down on the invaders.

Striking deceptively bad ice, Andy Cruickshank's plane was projected into the salty tide at the mouth of the Burnside River and plunged beneath the frigid waters—only to be miraculously brought back to the surface and re-conditioned by the "black gang," with the aid of Gus DeSteffany who taught them how to tie knots under freezing water. Less than half-way to Fort Resolution, Jimmie Spence was forced down on the frozen surface of Musk-ox Lake. Then, Roy Brown, making a forced landing while going to Spence's aid, had a wing-strut collapse, marooning him eighteen miles from his companion. Joining Spence, Roy and the mechanics spent two agonizing and desolate weeks wrapped in their bedrolls to maintain body temperature in the open tundra, vainly waiting for a rescue plane, while each alternately, braved the cold to prepare what little food there was for the others.

When the silvery tinkle of dog-bells reached the ears of the starved and half-frozen fliers, announcing the arrival of the relief dog-teams sent out by Andy Cruickshank from Fort Reliance on November 25th, it seemed indeed like a respite from doom.

Riding on the sleds, or slogging along on snowshoes behind the huskies they felt another surge of joy when the log walls of the lonely little outpost of Fort Reliance arose before them along the fringe of the tundra, the stove-pipes sending spirals of white vapour high into a coppery sky wherein sun-dogs warned of more stormy weather to come.

Immediately the rescued fliers were thawed out and properly looked after, then Andy headed across the wide expanse of Great Slave Lake through a chilling mist that rose from the open water and mingled with the drab obscurity overhead to Fort Resolution to announce their safe return, obtain spare parts, and prepare for the last long leg of the flight, via Stony Rapids, across the forested wilds of Northern Saskatchewan to The Pas.

By this time six of the rescue planes had been put out of commission, one having succumbed to the salty tide of Hudson Bay near Fort Churchill and become a total loss, while another—SK—had been left, tethered to a rock at Dease Point, in charge of Eskimos. Nearly a year later it was found in such perfect condition, despite the exposure, that the moment it was gassed-up and the pilot touched the controls it soared like an eagle into the air!

Not until December 3rd did the advance guard of the MacAlpine party reach The Pas. A cosmopolitan crowd of *capote*-clad Indians, trappers in traditional fringed buckskin and moccasins, townspeople muffled in fur coats, and the odd, smiling Celestial gathered at the landing field at Horace Halcrow Lake as the big Fokker settled easily upon the snow and proceeded to disgorge its human cargo.

Andy Cruickshank, Roy Brown, Dr. Bruce and Dick Pearce all appeared in good shape as they hopped out and acknowledged the hearty greetings of the crowd, but Don Goodwin, who had frozen his feet in the hazardous trek across the ice with the lost MacAlpine party to Cambridge Bay, had to be lifted into a taxi and taken to the hospital for an operation.

It was not until the entire party was snugly ensconced in the Fort Garry Hotel in Winnipeg a few days later that I learned from my old friend, Lockie Burwash, the inside story of what had actually happened to the Expedition from the time they disappeared from human ken at Baker Lake.

While at Fort Smith, Lockie had been the victim of one of those bitter and senseless Northern quarrels which seem, suddenly, to arise from no reasonable or coherent cause other than the long winter *ennui*, the clash of personalities as wide apart as the poles forced into the cramping environment of a small settlement, and personal jealousies. As a result, the Moguls at Ottawa—who knew nothing, and cared less, about local conditions—after mistakenly removing him from Fort Smith as administrator had, belatedly, recognized his worth by sending him on a one-man exploratory expedition into the Arctic which would have fazed many a younger man. But, Lockie was of tough fibre and wide experience. He made an outstanding success of a hazardous enterprise—capping it with his notable discoveries concerning the lost Franklin Expedition.

Having completed his jaunt across the roof of the world, he had seized upon the opportunity offered by the MacAlpine planes to fly back Outside, and it was my good fortune to renew old associations in Winnipeg, and hear his first-hand account of the experiences of Colonel MacAlpine and his men.

After leaving Baker on September 9th, the party had spent one night at Beverley Lake, and pushed on, despite extremely poor visibility as far as Pelly Lake. From there they planned to proceed north of Back's River, hitting Bathurst Inlet near Burnside River. Having learned that a large lake lay to the south of Bathurst, the leading pilot, on seeing a large body of water below, came to the conclusion that the line of flight passed south of the Inlet, whereas the sun compass showed this to be impossible. Still, there was a great deal of confusion since this body of water did not appear on the map. Leaving this unnamed lake, they ran into atrocious weather, which obscured the sun and made the use of the sun compass impossible, forcing them to resort to a *magnetic* compass—notoriously unreliable in such close proximity to the Magnetic Pole.

Knowing they were off-course, the party, after a long search for a suitable lake, came down to check on their position, their object being to reach the Arctic Ocean as soon as practicable. Taking the air again in the face of a snorting nor'wester they attained their object by making a safe landing on the barren reaches of Queen Maud Gulf, near a family of Cogmollock Eskimos.

Sea-ice began to appear near their camp on September 10th but, a couple of days later, flying weather improved sufficiently for them to make an abortive trip in search of a trading post which the Eskimo reported was situated three days' travel—approximately seventy-five miles—along the south shore, whereas Cambridge Bay Post actually lay across an arm of the sea, on the south-east shore of Victoria Land. By this time it was fully realized that, since the last of the gas had been exhausted in this futile search, there was no hope of flying, or sending, out by air for help.

Available rations, it was soon discovered, amounted to less than a hundred pounds, which meant curtailing the monthly issue to ten pounds per man to be on the side of safety.

There was only one thing to do: to make the best of a decidedly awkward and unpleasant situation, and to wait as patiently as their respective dispositions permitted, until Dease Strait should freeze over, permitting a dash over the sea-ice to the post at Cambridge Bay. Meanwhile, to augment distressingly slim pickings, they hunted ptarmigan, and the few Arctic hare they could find, and fished with varying success for tomcod.

Since tents proved cold and inadequate in the absence of tin stoves and stovepipes, they reared a rough house of stone and rubble, chinking it with moss. The primary problem was now fuel, and the Colonel set everyone to work digging up willow-roots and dry moss, which gave out more smoke than heat, necessitating their hugging their bedrolls when not working in a vain attempt to keep out the penetrating damp and cold.

When, on October 21st, they set out in a desperate attempt to end their miseries by heading out across the frozen Strait they discovered they had merely exchanged one type of wretchedness for another. Emaciated, and half-starved, they slipped and fell as shell-ice gave way under their weight, precipitating them into brine-filled holes that soaked their footgear—which immediately froze and chafed already sore feet. That night their igloo, built of soft snow, collapsed about their ears, necessitating them digging out their equipment in the darkness and re-building it as a protection from the biting blasts. By morning deep water covered the ice for miles, making further progress impossible. On the 24th they made a second start, only to run into similar conditions after negotiating twenty-five weary and frustrating miles.

By November 1st, with rations almost gone, they were reduced to eating frozen herring raw, their plight now being serious in the extreme—with leads opening up all around.

On November 3rd, they dragged themselves from their hastily-improvised igloo with the knowledge that, if they *didn't* win the last lap of their race with death that day, their hopes of survival were doomed. With feet torn and lacerated from the layers of salty slush that leaked into their footwear and froze into razor-like sharpness, they continued resolutely to place pain and fatigue behind them and struggle on in a long, gaping line over newly-formed ice that would not have supported any number of close-moving men. Suddenly, Dick Pearce pointed ahead. Through the semi-darkness of the Arctic night a thin, attenuated finger seemed to rise into the sky from what appeared to be still larger ice-hummocks.

"A ship's mast," growled the Colonel, "or I'm a Dutchman!"

It *was* the mast of the *Bay Maud*, and the "ice hummocks" soon resolved themselves into the white-painted buildings of the Hudson's Bay Company's post of Cambridge Bay!

With characteristic Northern hospitality, Paddy Gibson, the Company's trader, the Mounted Police, and the employees of the Canalaska Trading Company vied with each other in showering whatever comforts and help the little polar outpost was capable of furnishing upon the emaciated and trail-worn travellers. Within a couple of hours of their arrival all had partaken of a sumptuous meal, and been assigned real beds—the first they had slept on since the end of August—in trading posts, barracks, and aboard the *Bay Maud*, whence the magic words of the safety of the Expedition were wafted south by the Colonel to worrying wives and relatives.

In telling the story of the rescue of the MacAlpine party, the press waxed eulogistic concerning the heroism, courage and resourcefulness of the pilots who took their lives in their hands so frequently. But little, or nothing, was said of the equally perilous and outstanding work of the "black gang,"[2] those grease-begrimed mechanics who kept the planes aloft.

Under Tommy Siers, head mechanic and maintenance manager for Western Canada Airways, Graham Longley, Bill Nadin, Paul Davis, Pat

2. A phrase aptly coined by Alan Bill, then a Winnipeg *Tribune* reporter; now editor of the Calgary *Herald*.

Semple and Alf Walker performed miraculous feats in repairing the intricate mechanism of Fokkers and Fairchilds under bitter cold and harrassing weather conditions in the open tundra to keep them airworthy. They struggled without the tools that any ordinary mechanic would have demanded; without shelter, or any appropriate place in which to work; exposed continually to the elemental wrath of an unfriendly region, and the open sweep of the snow-covered Barrens. At times, indeed, they appeared to struggle without hope, yet succeeded in patching together airplanes that seemed irretrievably damaged.

"The whole story of the rescue flight," remarked Andy Cruickshank with heartfelt admiration, "is the story of miracles by mechanics. If it hadn't been for the 'black gang' the flight would have ended two weeks ago!"

There was the salvaging of Andy's plane from a watery grave in the depths of Burnside River, hoisting it back on the ice, and putting it back into service. Again, on Bathurst Inlet, a main bolt was broken when an undercarriage was torn off. Since replacing it anywhere within a thousand miles was out of the question, the mechanics improvised one from the handle of a wrench. The handle of a frying-pan replaced a broken strut; a magneto was repaired with some wire from an old radio, while, on another occasion, when two compression struts on the undercarriage of Jimmie Spence's plane buckled they were replaced by the tapering end of a steel wireless mast!

"All this newspaper talk about an epic flight and heroism," Roy Brown commented acidly to Winnipeg reporters, "is the bunk. We were just doing our jobs. Flying is what we are paid to do. The only unusual thing about it was that—*we were flying up there at a time we had no business to!*"

Meanwhile, concern was growing for another lost flier, missing somewhere amongst the snow-capped peaks and mighty glaciers of Alaska, which was to culminate in still another epic of the so-called "frozen frontier." When Carl Ben Eielson disappeared while on a rescue flight to carry succour to an American schooner, the *Nanuk*, caught in the grinding ice-floes off North Cape on the Siberian coast two hundred miles north of the Arctic Circle, the Aviation Corporation of New York picked on "Doc" Oaks to take charge of an aerial expedition to hunt for the missing Eielson.

Eielson, it was learned, had picked up a load of furs from the ice-locked schooner, delivered them safely, and was lost while returning to fly out the Captain and his pretty daughter. "Doc" had promptly selected as his pilots for this hazardous undertaking, Pat Reid and Gifford Swartzman, and mechanics Sam McAuley and Bill Hughes. Flying north to Fairbanks, Pat took off for Nome, only to disappear completely in the howling whiteness of a terrific nor'wester that blanketed peaks and valleys in a mantle of shimmering snow. Forced down by the suddenness and ferocity of the storm, Pat and his mechanic spent a week of frigid isolation in the heart of the snow-blanketed tundra, that had never seen a human footprint, repairing the wing damaged in the almost disastrous forced landing, only to re-appear in snow-bound Nome to the utter astonishment of both townsfolk and Eskimos, who had given them up for lost.

Showered with back-pattings and congratulations, Pat merely grinned, tuned up his plane and headed out over the endless miles of up-ended ice across the Bering Sea, knowing that, over this dangerous mass of moving floe-ice, unpredictable storms and fog-banks, a forced landing would mean certain death. Over along the rugged Siberian coast, Pat spotted, through the humming shrouds, the tangled wreckage of Eielson's plane. Picking up the frozen bodies of Eielson and his mechanic, he finally flew them back to Fairbanks.[3]

---

3. While the manuscript of this book was being prepared word was received of the tragic death of Pat Reid and his wife, along with thirty-five other passengers, when the ill-fated T.C.A. North Star airliner plunged to earth in flaming wreckage over the city of Moose Jaw, Saskatchewan, on April 8th, 1954, after a mid-air collision with an R.C.A.F. training plane.—P.H.G.

Note: During an official inspection of the Western Arctic District for the Hudson's Bay Company in 1923-1924, the author transferred the Company's headquarters from Herschel Island to Aklavic, a move immediately followed by Inspector Stuart T. Wood of the Mounted Police. Proceeding east to Coronation Gulf aboard the *Lady Kindersley*, the writer established Fort Brabant and Cambridge Bay posts on Victoria Island, and despatched a two-man expedition, consisting of Pete Norberg and Otto Torrington from the mouth of the Coppermine to King Williams Land and Boothia Peninsula. This expedition located 400 hitherto unknown Eskimos and established another trading post on King Williams Land, graveyard of the lost Franklin Expedition.—P.H.G.

8

PIONEERING THE ARCTIC AIR MAIL

I n preparation for another assault on the age-old barriers of the North to establish the first Government-sponsored air mail service from civilization to the Polar Sea, "Wop" May first decided to move his home to the frontier settlement of Fort McMurray, future headquarters for Commercial Airways on the 1,800 mile run to Aklavic.[1]

"Our home," Mrs. May recalls, "was a small frame building on the main street with a high, square false-front that gave it the appearance of a deserted store. Someone *did* tell me that it was an abandoned barber shop! But, dwellings of any kind were hard to get and we were more than glad to move in. There were three rooms, with a wood-burning heater in the front and middle ones, and a stove in the kitchen to keep the place warm. But the building was quite cold, and an inch of ice would form around the walls in the cold weather. We had outside plumbing, and our wood and water were hauled by Grant Owen. Our garbage was thrown into a deep pit where the loose huskies soon disposed of it. When they got too hungry for our scraps they often fell in, and we had quite a time hauling the frantic creatures out. We used gasoline lamps and, in the winter months, had to light up soon after three o'clock in the afternoon."

Mrs. May was delighted to find that she would have for a neighbour Walter Gilbert—who had just joined Western Canada Airways—and

1. In the summer of 1923, while inspecting the Western Arctic District, the writer decided to transfer the Hudson's Bay Company's headquarters from Herschel Island to Scenic (now known as Aklavic). The advantages were numerous: contact with the outside world was more frequent; wood and timber were available for fuel, building and protection, while the extension of the sternwheeler route from Ft. McPherson to Aklavic brought in sight the abandonment of the hazardous Bering Sea supply route in favour of surer transportation down the Mackenzie River, and the distribution of Western Arctic freight along the Arctic coast by small schooners. Stuart T. Wood, R.C.M.P. Inspector at Herschel Island, destined later to become Commissioner, warmly welcomed my suggestion and promptly moved Royal Mounted Police Headquarters to Aklavic also.

Prior to this it had been necessary for the entire staffs of the Hudson's Bay Company and the Mounted Police, together with books, prisoners and even huskie dogs, to abandon Herschel Island and move over on the last ice in May to Ft. McPherson or Arctic Red River, there to await the arrival of the sternwheeler with mail in mid-July; after which all would return by motor schooner in time to reach Herschel Island before the ships arrived from Seattle and Vancouver in August. Thus Aklavic became, forthwith, the commercial and administrative centre of the Western Arctic. This gipsying back and forth became a thing of the past. The uncertain Bering Sea route was abandoned in favour of the Mackenzie River transport route and, as such, it still remains, with the strong probability that its rapid growth will necessitate Aklavic's removal ere long to higher ground.—P.H.G.

his wife, Jeanne, who flew in from Edmonton in the teeth of a mounting blizzard on January 1st, 1930, in one of the new Fokker Super-Universals, then the latest thing in aircraft for Arctic flight.

At first the Gilberts acquired a room in the Franklin Hotel, where warm-hearted Mrs. O'Coffey delighted in mothering the girlish pioneer. Aided by the redoubtable Dr. Ings, who had once been house physician to Queen Liluokalani of Hawaii, the Gilberts were soon housed in a two-roomed wooden shack behind the hotel, and enjoyed with Mrs. May all the thrills and discomforts of pioneer life.

With his frontier home established, "Wop" lost no time in preparing for the long flight ahead. At Fort McMurray and Edmonton reposed five tons of mail, including 125,000 letters destined for the northern fur posts, missions and Mounted Police barracks along the mighty chain of rivers leading to the terminus of Aklavic, only sixty miles from the Polar Sea. In the past this vast region had been dependent upon slow-moving dog-teams that relayed only letter mail from one fur fort to another, the through trip from Fort McMurray to Aklavic usually consuming a couple of months—parcels and newspapers being permitted to pile up till the first stern-wheelers headed north after the opening of navigation in the summer. Now everything— parcels, letters and newspapers—were to be flown to the news-hungry exiles.

In preparation for the flight three Bellancas and the Lockheed Vega had been tuned-up at Blatchford Field in Edmonton since December 1st, awaiting favourable weather conditions to head into the blue. Meanwhile, "Wop," as senior pilot of the Red Armada, had headed north to Fort McMurray in the flagship, one of the three Bellancas he had ferried west from New York, to make advance preparations for the take-off.

As though to challenge this new adventure in aviation, Keewatin— God of the North Wind—had unleashed his furies with biting blasts that sent the thermometer reeling to 49° below zero, effectively grounding Idris Glyn Roberts, former R.A.F. pilot; Cy Becker, pilot-manager of Commercial Airways; Pilot Lumsden, and Tim Sims— mechanic and air-expert on Wright engines. Not until noon,

Walter Gilbert.
Glenbow Archives NA-463-6

December 9th, was Cy Becker able to lead the two Bellancas and the stream-lined Lockheed Vega northward, to alight beside "Wop's" plane on the frozen snye at Fort McMurray. By morning bitter weather, and visibility that seemed to reach no higher than the poplar-lined tops of the riverbank, again kept the air-fleet grounded, and not until Wednesday did "Wop" head his flagship down the long, white reaches of the Athabasca, with the rest of the air-fleet riding in the rear, trailing long tendrils of white vapour in the frosty sky.

At last "Wop" was heading into the heart of that mysterious land of romance and adventure—the Mackenzie-Athabasca valley—whose foundations had been laid a century-and-a-half before by that swashbuckling Connecticut Yankee, Peter Pond, and those rollicking, hard-fighting, hard-drinking Nor'Westers in the days when the Hudson's Bay Company's factors were still hugging their mud fireplaces beside the storm-tossed waters of Hudson Bay.

Clinging like birds' nests to the riverbank, a hundred-and-fifty to two hundred miles apart, are the fur posts—the commercial centres of the land—each in the centre of a small clearing surrounded on three sides by the primeval forest, and fronted by the mile-wide reaches of the frozen Mackenzie and the Athabasca. Each so-called fort consisted of a huddle of mudded, log buildings, with an encircling picket-fence, or palisade, and the inevitable flagpole flaunting its red ensign emblazoned with the letters "H.B.C."—variously interpreted as "Hudson's Bay Company," "Here Before Christ," or, by those who loved not the great commercial company, as "The Halfbreed's Curse."

The unutterable loneliness of these little outposts of civilization struck the newcomer forcibly. Cut off for nine months in the year before the coming of the commercial aeroplane, the life was one of ineffable solitude yet, at steamer time, they managed to surround themselves with a brief gala spirit. With the hunters in from the woods, the trappers and camp traders lounging about in quiet contentment bartering their fur hunts, or helping the factors bale up the accumulated wealth of the winter for shipment to distant London or New York, and the clearings dotted with the conical tepees of the tawny tribesmen who, from the surrounding forests, amassed the peltries with which the wheels of commerce were kept revolving, these posts presented a vastly different appearance from what they did in winter. Then the Indian and half-breed hunters were scattered far and wide in the snow-mushroomed forests; the frozen river became a mass of piled-up *bordeaux*; the whole world was buried under a deep blanket of shimmering whiteness, and the traders, jealous and distrustful of each other, barely spoke when they passed on the trail.

In many respects there had been re-enacted amongst these solitudes conditions almost identical with those that had existed in the valley of the St. Lawrence in the picturesque days of the French regime. The autocratic control which had characterized the former rule of the Fur Lords had been followed by the ascendency of the Roman Catholic Church, whose cassocked priests and self-abnegating nuns in their log-walled missions had become the pivot around which nearly all the aboriginal life revolved. For, just as the resolute and fearless Father Rale had gathered his Abenaki converts around him in their squalid cabins upon the rocky shores of Maine, and Brébeuf and Lalemant had erected their bark churches amongst the Hurons of Ontario three centuries before, so had the courageous Oblate Fathers in the twentieth century persuaded the motley tribesmen of the Mackenzie to forsake, to some extent, their nomadic pursuit of the caribou to form permanent settlements around their wooden churches.

It was Walter Hale,[2] the "Flying Postmaster," rather than "Wop" who saw these conditions in their true perspective. As they headed into the heavy snowstorm that whipped the mail planes with clouds of spinning flakes visibility was reduced to nil, forcing the seasoned pilot to the grim necessity of "flying by the seat of his pants." This latter variety of flying must have proven strikingly effective for, just as the purple light that precedes darkness was creeping into the white curtain of falling flakes, "Wop" brought the *Lady Edmonton* to an almost effortless landing beneath the red-grey rocks atop which ancient Fort Chipewyan—the Athens of the Northwest and cradle of discovery—stood silent sentinel.

2. Colonel Walter Hale made his first trip into the North by scow in the fall of 1921 in company with the author and his wife.—P.H.G.

As the *Solway*, the *Mills* and the Lockheed Vega descended in cascades of swirling snow and nosed down to a landing, cowled figures in hairy caribou-skin *parkas* slipped silently on moccasined feet down the snow-drifted rock ramparts in a mingling of Chipewyan, French and English. The leader of the reception committee proved to be a sturdy, dark-visaged half-breed, John James Loutitt, the Hudson's Bay factor, who extended a guttural welcome to the hospitality of the "Gentlemen Adventurers." Then a tall, spare, alert man, very dark of countenance, with silvery hair and lively black eyes, shook hands all around. It was the veteran, Colin Fraser, whose appearance belied the fact that he was well on towards his eighties. In the veins of this ancient "free trader," who had long been a thorn in the Company's side, coursed the blood of Blackfoot, Cree and Highland Scot. The grandson, and namesake, of the Colin Fraser who had been Piper to Sir George Simpson, the Little Emperor of Rupert's Land, his proudest possession was the bagpipes which had been used to announce the arrival and departure of this wilderness potentate at the forts throughout the land.

Declining Colin's generous offer to visit his post and join in a few rounds of sloe gin, "Wop," Glyn Roberts and Walter Hale climbed the rocks to the Hudson's Bay post, set out in the conventional square surmounted by a long, tapering flagpole from which, despite the lateness of the hour, the scarlet banner of the Hudson's Bay Company fluttered out its salutation.

Behind the post, contrasting boldly with the green of the spruce, towered the spires and turrets of the Roman Catholic Mission, where others of the party found hospitable billets for the night.

Grounded, next morning, by poor visibility and recurrent blasts of drifting snow, "Wop" accompanied Walter Hale on a tour of the historic trading post which Alexander Mackenzie had used as a base for his two great voyages of discovery—down the Mackenzie to the Polar Sea, and overland to the Pacific Ocean.

"Reminds me of old Fort Edmonton," "Wop" said, gazing around the square of massive log buildings, "and of the times Court and I used to pry bullets out of the log walls there with our jackknives!"

There was little, however, to connect it with its earlier history as the palisades, the watchtower, and most of the old landmarks were gone. Within the warehouses were piled furs, caribou skins, dried meat, and the usual assortment of painted dog-*carrioles,* toboggans, dog-harness, and beaded *tapis* and standing-irons. Upon the shelves of the low-beamed trading store were the everyday Hudson's Bay blankets, gaudy *L'Assomption* sashes, powder-horns, muzzle-loaders, kettles and other articles of commerce.

The atmosphere of earlier days was, however, recalled by the old *Journals* lying promiscuously about, a veritable gold mine for the historian. Glancing at random through one of these, "Wop" came across an entry bearing the date of May 22nd, 1831, which proved that cannibalism was not infrequent in the "good old days."

"They, the Crees," he read aloud, "bring intelligence that Moussitoussicapo is at their tent, having lately joined them without his family of two women and two children, who perished during the winter. From his frequent prevarications when questioned by the other Crees, they suspect he has murdered and devoured them."

"Look at this," Walter Hale chuckled as he glanced at the neat copperplate of some Hudson's Bay clerk long dead and gone and caught another insight upon the trader's point of view with regard to his aboriginal charges:

June 19, 1831. Two Chipewyans came from the Long Point informing us that Big Head's son is dead, that Big Head has thrown away his property in consequence of the loss of his boy, and that he told them to beg a shirt and tobacco. The shirt, of course, I did not send; the scoundrel is not worthy of it. I merely sent him six inches of tobacco with reluctance. That cursed family is a perfect pest to the place, and it is my humble opinion that the hand of Providence sends them the present calamity for their ill deeds.

Something of the spirit and steadfastness of that ghostly company of adventurers who had reared this outpost of Empire in the wilderness—Peter Pond, Alexander Mackenzie, and their successors, Franklin and Rae—seemed to arise from the leaves of these diaries, spotted with the grease of candles made from buffalo-tallow and the fingerprints of factors and clerks of long ago.

"Those Nor'Wester boys must have had some guts," commented Hale as they gazed across the snow-covered lake, with its clusters of pine-clad islands, towards the site of the original stronghold at Old Fort Point, five miles away. "Imagine hauling goods—and *rum*," he chuckled, "three thousand miles by canoe from Montreal to here to cut off these Indians from the Hudson's Bay posts on Hudson Bay! No wonder they watered down the rum once they got it this far!"

"Too bad they haven't some of that rum here now," "Wop" laughed. "You know," he hazarded, "I've always had a soft spot in my heart for Peter Pond. *He* was the one who did the pioneering. He was the first to cross the height of land; the first to build a post here and break the sod—and got the least out of it! I've always had a hunch that Mackenzie built his success on the detraction of that old rascal, Pond, and on *his* geographical discoveries. Why, Pond even reported on the coal deposits at the Peace River Canyon, called it the 'Carboniferous River.' And, don't forget—it was Peter Pond who overcame transportation problems by introducing the use of *pemmican* as a light, sure and concentrated food to ration his canoemen. Transportation's always been the problem that held this country back. Maybe," "Wop" flashed one of his enigmatic smiles, "it'll remain for us, Walter, to beat it? Imagine, only a short while ago, in the York boat days, it took *eight years* from the time the Company's goods left England before the furs traded for these same goods got back to London!"

Not till Friday morning did the weather clear sufficiently to permit the Red Armada to take to the skies and head northward towards Fort Fitzgerald. With Walter Hale beside him, "Wop" gazed down on the unfolding panorama as the mighty *Unjigah*, or Peace River, joined forces with the forest-lined Athabasca to become, thenceforth, known as the Slave—a name that had originated from the Crees when they overran the Athabasca country, driving the frightened Slaves northward to Great Slave Lake—there to be mercilessly butchered on Dead

Man's Island. At the mouth of the Peace the warring tribes had finally gathered to inhale the fragrance of *kinnikinnick* and seal a peace that was to be perpetuated in the name of the river. As his eyes swept the landscape below he beheld, for the first time, wild buffalo grazing placidly along the banks, and amongst the patches of snow-covered meadow. At first he couldn't make out the composition of the black moving blotches that mottled the whiteness of the snow in spots and turned an inquiring glance on Walter.

"Buffalo!" Hale exclaimed, leaning forward in his seat for a better view. "There used to be two distinct herds, separated by a wide strip of muskeg. The northern herd numbered around thirteen-hundred and the southern herd about twelve-hundred," he shouted above the roar of the engine, "though, at one time, old-timers estimated them as low as three-hundred. A few years ago the Government shipped down six-thousand prairie buffalo by scow from Fort McMurray and turned them loose on that range below. Many of them were two-year-olds, and they made a frantic attempt to get back to the dry prairie land to which they'd been accustomed and died, or were drowned, while others were killed by the heavier wood buffalo, who resented their intrusion. They say," Walter added as the plane soared high into the skies, "that there's ten-thousand[3] of these mixed buffalo on the 17,300 square mile Wood Buffalo Park preserve. But—your guess is as good as mine!"

At last, the squalid trading post of Fort Fitzgerald appeared below, its long waterfront littered with dead trees, broken scows, rotting canoes and discarded machinery, to say nothing of a line of ramshackle log cabins belonging to the Caribou Eater tribe—the *Etheneldeli*, or Rising Sun People, as they called themselves—whose ancestors had traded with Samuel Hearne at the old stone stronghold of Fort Prince of Wales on Hudson Bay.

Between here and Fort Smith, the so-called capital of the Northwest Territories, sixteen miles away, lay the only obstruction to navigation from Fort McMurray to the Polar Sea—a portage road having been

3. Now, 1954, estimated at 15,000.

slashed through the forest by the fur traders to circumvent Pelican Rapids, Mountain Rapids, and the Rapids of the Drowned where two priests had perished. Atop the rocks overlooking the rapids a towering white cross commemorated the tragic event. A line of rickety Red River carts hitched to scrawny cayuses had carried the freight across in the summer time from the steamers plying on the upper river to the *Mackenzie River* and the *Distributor*, which plied to the Arctic. As the plane descended, billowing clouds of frosty vapour rose in chilling splendour from the open rapids into the frigid skies above.

Feeling somewhat like a knight in shining armour in his hairy *parka*, fringed duffle leggings and moose-skin moccasins, Walter Hale expected an ovation from the straggling line of fur-clad humans who descended upon the pioneer air-mail planes. Instead, he was greeted with a storm of withering abuse by the spokesman, Sid Leggo.

"What the hell," blustered the ubiquitous, round-faced and chubby factor from Fort Smith, "has been keeping you so long? Here it is, the 12th of December, and we've been expecting you for ten days! A *dog-team* could have made the trip in the time you birds have taken!"

"Sure," Percy Round interjected. "And with the old dog-team you knew to a *day*, almost to the hour, when they'd arrive. Now—nobody knows nuthin'! Gimme the old dog-team any old day. To *hell* with these new contraptions!"

Whipping out of the cockpit in time to gather the import of the "welcoming" committee's remarks, "Wop" rose belligerently to the occasion. "We've been held up by bad weather," his voice was like a whip-lash. "Now, tell me—where in hell are those dog-teams that were to meet us here with the Fort Smith mail? I suppose we'll have to land three miles below there, beyond the bad ice at the foot of the rapids, and *haul* your goddamned mail down there on our backs!"

Nervously, Sid wiped his thick-lensed glasses. "I . . . I guess . . .," he countered lamely, "they must be half-way across the Portage by this time!"

By the time the overdue dog-teams appeared, and snaked across the ice to the waiting plane, it was already turning dusk, and further flying for the day was out of the question.

Taking off from Fort Fitzgerald the following morning while the light was still dim, the big monoplanes headed for Fort Resolution on Great Slave Lake, gateway to the land of the caribou and the prehistoric musk-oxen. By steering a straight course across the Wood Buffalo Park and emerging at the mouth of the Little Buffalo, "Wop" planned to cut the one-hundred-and-seventy-five mile trail along the Slave River to an hour-and-a-half's flying time. The thermometer stood at ten-below, with a north wind that remained constant even at 10,000 feet, by long odds the greatest altitude achieved by the planes to date. Except for the first ten minutes of the flight, when the ships were cutting through the chill mists rising from the open rapids at Smith Portage, travelling was pleasant.

Frederick Watt of the Edmonton *Journal*, who accompanied the fliers, wrote:

Forty-five minutes after the take-off the sunrise created a sight that, at 9,000 feet, was breath-taking in its magnificence. To the south, the mists that cloaked half the great circle of the horizon were shot through with brilliant rays from blood-red to every colour of the rainbow.

Never have I seen a lovelier riot of colour. To the west were banks of clouds floating at 5,000 feet, stretched to the skyline like a fiery eiderdown quilt. The Slave River wound its tortuous way between banks of snow rims which glinted like silver in the sunlight. Even the most unimpressionable members of the party were compelled to remark on the beauty of the scene.

On the last stage of the trip where the river swings to the east, May led the Red Armada directly across country to a height of over 10,000 feet. From this altitude it was possible to see the junction of the Slave River and the lake, more than fifty miles distant.

Approaching our destination engines were throttled down and the scarlet arrow descended in a long series of glides that ended five hundred feet above the frozen lake. As we banked over the fort a large red Hudson's Bay flag was run up on a tall flagpole from a palisaded square of log buildings near the edge of the lake, its vivid folds waving a cheery welcome that contrasted sharply with the glistening white background and the dark green conifers.

The runway on the ice proved to be in very fair shape and within a few minutes all three ships were drawn up in line before the fort while the entire population of *parka*-clad traders, led by Carl Murdoff of the Northern Traders, black-gowned priests and Mounted Police, to say nothing of an array of mahogany-faced Yellow-Knife and Slavey tribesmen whose squaws remained modestly in the background, cascaded down on to the ice and surrounded the fleet in an admiring circle.

Carl Murdoff, the local postmaster, promptly threatened to conscript both Becker and Hale to assist in sorting the 1,750 pounds of mail the dog-teams finally freighted from the mail planes to his office in the Northern Trading store.

Meanwhile, Corporal Lorne Halliday of the Mounted Police, scarlet serge jettisoned for a hooded caribou-skin *parka*, was heading a dog-team laden with four hundred pounds of mail across the frigid reaches of Great Slave Lake for Fort Rae, the small but important Hudson's Bay post perched on a rocky promontory a hundred-and-seventy-five miles to the eastward in the Land of Little Sticks—hunting grounds of the still primitive Dog-Rib tribesmen.

Beautiful weather made the flight across Great Slave Lake to Hay River, with its Hudson's Bay post, Anglican Mission, and Indian and Eskimo school, the most pleasant travelling so far experienced. In fact, it was much too pleasant in the air for Pilots May and Becker, whose engines were adjusted to more severe temperatures. The mighty lake, greater in size than Lake Erie, stretching in illimitable whiteness to the horizon, presented an aspect of ethereal beauty as it whisked past below "Wop's" flagship. Until a week before the water was frozen only half a mile from shore. But the bitter weather, experienced while awaiting the initial take-off from Edmonton to Fort McMurray, had closed the great central sheet of open water and the glare ice, uncovered as yet by snow, stretched in an immense turquoise blanket as far as the eye could reach north and east.

The Rev. B. Singleton of the Anglican Mission at Hay River greeted the appearance of the mail planes with warm enthusiasm as the vast array of mail-sacks was discharged upon the frozen river.

At this post there were more white women than at any fort along the Mackenzie, most of them engaged in the somewhat dubious task of teaching young Indians and Eskimos the Three R's and a smattering of English. Literally kidnapped from their families for a space of ten years, these youngsters were *un*taught everything Indian and Eskimo they might need later on to wrest a living from the forests and along the barren Arctic coast, a policy which resulted in their developing a wholesome contempt for everything Indian and Eskimo which, in some cases, applied even to their own parents.

Following lunch, the fliers were treated by Mr. Middleton to a lusty rendition of popular hymns by a chorus of dusky young Chipewyan, Slavey and Eskimo proselytes who might have been better employed learning to snare rabbits, or hunting seal and caribou.

From the palisaded post of Fort Providence, at the commencement of the *true* Mackenzie River, where Fred McLeod, whose brothers had gone to their deaths in Dead Man's Valley to the westward, presided as factor for the Hudson's Bay Company, it was but a short hop to "Head of the Line," the point where erstwhile *voyageurs* had exchanged sails and oars, after the arduous task of hauling fur-laden *batteaux*, or York boats, with a long, wavering tow-line the thousand-odd miles from Fort Good Hope and Fort McPherson. At length they looked down upon Fort Simpson, rising in lofty aloofness from a pine-clad island set at the spot where the troubled Liard debouches into the majestic, high-banked Mackenzie.

Once the headquarters for the Mackenzie River District, Fort Simpson, like Fort Chipewyan, had been the cradle of exploration for the rugged interior. Here, Chief Factor Julian Camsell—the "Glass-eyed God of the Mackenzie" as the bespectacled little man was known to the Klondykers—had ruled in almost feudal state. Now, however, the fort had degenerated in both standing and appearance but, to the airmen, it held a special interest since it was here, in 1921, that Captain Gorman had come to grief with the first two Junkers to assail the

North. To the westward, the burnished summits of the sinister Nahannie Mountains tusked the sky in lordly aloofness.

It was a lonely and austere land, completely cut-off till now from the outside world in winter save for the occasional dog-teams that threaded the two thousand miles of frozen river and forest, bringing the mail, such as it was, from the end-of-steel at Fort McMurray. North and south skin-clad Dog-Ribs and tawny Chipewyan and Slavey Indians roamed the forests as did their ancestors, hunting the antlered moose, and toiling on webbed snowshoes beneath the ghostly scintillations of the *aurora borealis* to trap beaver, lynx, marten, mink and silver foxes, and barter their pelts at the scattered forts along the frozen rivers. Once in a while a lone Mountie from one of the isolated fur forts would patrol the snow-bound wilderness with his Indian guide and team of sharp-eared huskies, but the Mounted Police were few and far between.

Here, at Fort Simpson, crews and passengers filled tanks in a temperature of seventy-below zero. As elsewhere, the moment a plane landed, the oil had to be drained immediately to prevent it from freezing solid in the engine. Before the aircraft took off it had to be heated and poured back, hot, since an idle engine's lubrication freezes solid in a few minutes in these frigid latitudes.

Gasoline barrels had to be located deep in mountainous drifts of frozen snow. The barrels had to be rolled to the planes, tanks filled, and the engines overhauled. And, handling gas in seventy-below weather from metal drums was anything but a sinecure. Often the overhaul meant that pilots and mechanics had to work bare-handed, using heated tools.

In the dim, diffused dawn-light, after arrival at one of these posts, there was always the walk back from the trading post to the plane; hours spent kindling fires in the bush, heating oil, and keeping blow-torches going beneath the engine. So intense was the cold at times that it actually put out the torch, while, at all times, someone had to stand guard with a fire extinguisher lest the inflammable machine be ignited by a wayward spark.

When engine and oil reached the right heat there was a mad rush to scramble aboard since, when the temperature drops to fifty-below, not a moment can be lost in embarkation lest the engine cool off and the whole warming-up procedure have to be repeated.

Hopes of the northern air-mail reaching Aklavic at the end of the route by Christmas received a decided set-back when the *Lady Edmonton*, carrying the full consignment of mail for Fort Wrigley, Fort Norman and Fort Good Hope, was forced to return to Fort Simpson fifteen minutes after taking off. A short distance down-river a dense wall of swirling snow had been encountered, causing "Wop" May to head back in time to prevent the two remaining Bellancas starting out on their hop back to Fort Resolution. Hard on the tail of the retreating *Lady Edmonton* came the death-blow to the day's hopes in the shape of a shrieking northern blizzard.

Two days before Christmas, under a sky that remained overcast, and a temperature of sixty degrees below zero, the three Bellancas took off from Fort Simpson at daylight for points separated by more than a thousand miles. "Wop" May headed the *Lady Edmonton*, loaded with mail for diminutive Fort Wrigley, deep in the snow-capped mountains, and Fort Norman. Glyn Roberts swung the nose of the *Mills* towards Fort Resolution to ferry back the last load of the inaugural mail shipment, whilst Lumsden, in the *Solway*, started on the long trek to Fort McMurray to maintain the regular air-mail schedule at the more southerly forts. No reports would henceforth be heard of the flagship until its return to Fort Simpson since it was to cover the eight hundred mile stretch of the Mackenzie River, still unserved by wireless.

May took off while the cloud of snow raised by Harold Farrington's departure in a Western Canada Airways Fokker still hung in the air, and the two planes were swallowed up to the north.

Passing Mount Camsell, at the confluence of the North Nahannie, of evil repute, "Wop" soon found himself winging his way over towering mountain ranges that seemed to shrink the mighty Mackenzie into the appearance of a serpentine white thread until he put the ship down on bumpy ice and shook hands with the giant, six-foot-six French-Canadian factor, Tim Gaudet, at the little, three-cabin fort that seemed dwarfed into insignificance by its mountainous setting and the granite pile of Wrigley Rock. Here, at Fort Wrigley, Tim was almost an institution, and conducted the Company's fur trading activities with the primitive Mountain, or Nahannie, Indians.

Taking leave of the kindly and hospitable Tim, "Wop" flew a hundred and fifty miles to the northward, over the mountains that still smoke from the burning coal deposits as they did when first seen by Alexander Mackenzie a century and a half before. Beyond *Castor Debuille*, Bear Rock rose in lofty silhouette against a background of lemon and scarlet sunset, the flagship being suddenly obscured by a fog that descended upon the hummocky river ice. Sneaking its way through a hole in the fog, the plane had hardly skimmed the ice near the unimpressive settlement of Fort Norman before Glyn Roberts just missed making a three-point landing directly on top of "Wop's" ship.

The back-door to Great Bear Lake, and the land of Stefansson's so-called "blonde" Eskimos, it had seen Fathers Rouvier and LeRoux leave with high hopes to carry the Cross to these heathen Cogmollocks, only to fall before the copper snow-knives of these small, Tartar-faced savages in skin swallow-tails. Others—traders and Mounted Police—had also passed through its portal to meet death at the hands of these Stone Age savages on the icy reaches of the Polar Sea.

Over a bottle of Old Black rum, "Wop" listened avidly as old-timers related first-hand stories of Corporal Doak of the Mounted Police who had left there to become a victim of Cogmollock ferocity; of Captain Christian Klengenberg, the twentieth-century buccaneer who had cruised away with the stolen *Olga*, disposed of four of his crew who didn't see eye to eye with his piracy, and ended by discovering the "blonde" Eskimos, *six years before Stefansson ever laid eyes upon them;* and of Inspector Denny LaNauze's ten thousand mile patrol by way of Fort Norman to capture Sinissiak and Uluksuk, the slayers of Fathers Rouvier and LeRoux.

Though "Wop" little realized it at the time, it was to fall to the lot of himself, Leigh Brintnell and other budding bush-pilots to blaze new air-trails into the heart of the bleak and desolate Great Bear Lake region that lay in frigid isolation to the eastward and rear upon its granite rocks the boom towns of Eldorado and Port Radium, whence radium-bearing ore would be flown through the northern skies for processing at Port Hope, Ontario.

Another Northern tragedy was unfolded before the bush-fliers at this point. Walter Hale had brought along a suitable Christmas gift for the renowned trader, "Rags" Wilson, who was located at Good Hope Bay, a hundred miles to the east of the fort. Whilst trying to locate a dog-team leaving for the Bay, Walter discovered that "Rags" was actually in Fort Norman. His frozen body had been brought in the night before by dog-team after he had succumbed to a heart attack at his lonely post! Standing around the mortal remains of the popular and colourful trader, a silent toast was drunk to his memory from the very bottle that would have brightened his lonely Christmas.

It was at Fort Good Hope, two hundred miles north of Fort Norman, where the Mackenzie is compressed between the high rock walls of The Ramparts into a quarter of its normal width, that "Wop" came into contact with one of the Northland's most unique characters next day. From the group of hooded traders, Mounted Police and Hare Indians who had assembled to welcome the plane there emerged a thick-set, active man of about sixty with a decided Irish brogue. Of medium height, as powerful as an ox, he was attired in a home-made khaki suit of semi-military cut that fitted where it touched, a pair of beaded moccasins, and a battered nautical cap set awkwardly atop his shaven pate. It was immediately obvious that here was a personage of more than usual importance who expected to be treated with becoming deference. At first glance, "Wop" was completely fascinated by the man's unbelievable ugliness, his atrocious squint and low, receding forehead which gave him the appearance of Neanderthal Man.

"This is Mr. Flynn Harris," explained a young Mountie. "Our Indian Agent and Magistrate!"

Flynn shot his face aggressively forward until his nose was within an inch of "Wop's," closely scrutinized his visage with one of his swivel eyes, leered diabolically and swung his cap to the snow with a sweeping bow.

"My dear fellow—my *very* dear fellow—I am, indeed, honoured and charmed to meet the redoubtable *Captain* May. *Positively* delighted. Er! ... er! ... eh! ... as His Majesty's representative, permit me to welcome you to Fort Good Hope. It is, unfortunately, my dear sir, a very *dry* place at the moment. But," his gaze flitted hopefully towards the cabin of the *Lady Edmonton,* "I have hopes there will be a decided improvement in the humidity of the atmosphere with your arrival, and that the drought which we have endured for some time is nearly over—especially since this happens to be *Christmas* day. Do you ... er! speak Esperanto, Captain May?"

"Good God, no!" "Wop" ejaculated, wondering what would come next and signing to his mechanic to dig up a bottle of rum—still not sure as to which of the Magistrate's eyes was looking into his own. "I'm sorry, Mr. Harris, but I don't."

"Tut ... tut ... don't apologize," Flynn smiled affably as he led the procession up the high cutbank. "That is one of the misfortunes of living in such a God-forsaken place. Personally, I have always excelled in languages. Speak *eight* of them, you know: English, German, Spanish, Cree—my, er, wife's native tongue—Chipewyan and one or two others, including the dead languages and, of course, Esperanto. But one *does* get out of practice at a place like this, you know. But for the continual solace afforded me by my esteemed and intimate friend, John Barleycorn, I can assure you, Captain May, I should have been one of Canada's leading criminal lawyers. Sir Robert Borden, the former Premier, and I were school chums. Ah! my dear fellow, you must excuse me. There's my wife. These little courtesies, you know—they cost *so* little!"

Whereupon the voluble and flowery Mr. Harris bowed deeply to a dark-visaged Indian woman attired in a tartan galaplaid shawl, voluminous rose-pink skirt, black velvet blouse and moccasins, then presented her to "Wop" as "Caroline!"

"I would appreciate, very much, the honour of having you grace my board, but I must warn you," he gestured towards his wife with mittened hand, "I always insist on Caroline sitting with us at the table. I know it *isn't* done. She is a native. In fact, she's a *Chipewyan* squaw, but—I've found her good enough to live with, she has borne me my children, and I consider sir, that she's good enough to sit with me and my friends at the table."

Flynn cocked his chin aggressively, squinted at his short vile-smelling cutty-pipe and, with an anticipatory smile, eagerly reached for the bottle brought up by the mechanic.

Such was "Wop's" introduction to one of the most colourful and unique characters in the North. Actually, Flynn Harris was an outstanding Greek scholar and a master of eight languages, including Esperanto, and would, undoubtedly, have made a name for himself in legal circles but for his love of adventure, and an abiding affection for John Barleycorn which had bestowed upon him a somewhat chequered career.

When the annual liquor permits arrived with the opening of navigation, his affected politeness towards his wife went into reverse with a vengeance, while his pet epithet for his hybrid son was: "You little sod!" More than one visitor to his office, unaware of his idiosyncrasies when in his cups, had been embarrassed, to say the least, when Flynn insisted on conducting business in his birthday suit!

When the stream of liquid conviviality dried up, Flynn admitted to a partiality for *red ink*, both as a stimulant and a pick-me-up. When the Commissioner once queried his requisition for five gallons of red ink while he was in charge of the lonely and diminutive post at Fond du Lac—where a year's bookkeeping could be done in a day—Flynn had indignantly scrawled across one corner of the letter: "What I don't use I *abuse!*", and returned it to the head office.

Earlier on the trip preparations had been made to celebrate Christmas wherever it might overtake them in the wilderness, and stowed away in "Wop's" plane was a turkey, mince pies, canned sausages, and a quantity of bottled merriment. An empty and diminutive log Indian house, which seemed just a little colder than the prevailing sixty-seven below temperature without, was commandeered, and, by borrowing from the Mounted Police, the Mission and local traders a stove, stove-pipes, wood for a table and a few chairs, order gradually emerged from chaos. Ere long "Wop," Glyn Roberts, engi-

neers Tim Sims and Van der Linden, along with the ebullient Walter
Hale and Fred Watt, the reporter, were revelling in the heat thrown out
by the panting, red-hot stove wherein a fire now crackled merrily.

Already a couple of bottles of fiery Old Buck rum had been
broached and, despite the fact that it, like everything else, was frozen,
and poured as thick as molasses, nobody showed any disposition to
pass it up. While the fliers and mechanics defrosted themselves, exter-
nally and internally, the turkey was tossed into the oven, and bannock
and butter placed below to thaw. Jerking open a grimy flour-sack,
"Wop" ejected a black object that resembled a cannon-ball as it
bounced heavily across the floor.

"There you are, Walter," he grinned, "go ahead and cut this
Christmas cake!"

Despite the primitive surroundings an aura of festive hilarity pre-
vailed as Slim Rader and a scattering of lean-faced, *parka*-clad trappers, in from the surrounding forests, joined in the general hubbub. A
tall, attenuated Mountie was telling of his last Christmas dinner with
an old trapper—*stewed skunk*, washed down with execrable home-
brew—when Slim Rader waved a bottle over his head and burst into
song:

There's a husky, dusky maiden in the Arctic,
In her igloo she is waiting there in vain,
And some day I'll put my mukluks on and ask her
If she'll wed me when the Ice Worms nest again.

Howls of applause greeted the opening verse of *The Song of the
North*, brought across the Yukon divide by Slim Behn at the time of
the oil rush; then a loud, stentorian chorus followed in a medley of
hoarse keys:

In the Land of Pale Blue Snow,
Where it's ninety-nine below.
And the polar bears are roamin' o'er the plain,
In the shadow of the Pole

I'll clasp her to my soul,
We'll be happy when the Ice Worms nest again.

"Here! gimme a drink!" roared a backwoods impresario as he grabbed a bottle and tossed down a mighty drink to the accompaniment of the blood-chilling ululations of the huskie dogs roaming around outside.

Our wedding feast will be seal oil and blubber,
In our kayaks we will roam the boundless main.
How the walruses will turn their heads and rubber,
We'll be happy when the Ice Worms nest again.

"Where the hell's the turkey?" yelled "Wop," making a dash for the stove. A hasty examination of the *pièce de resistance* disclosed the fact that, while the defunct bird sported sundry water blisters and burned patches, it was still frozen solid in the centre, and would probably take another couple of hours of semi-incineration to cook. Yanking it from the pan, he attacked it with an axe, tossed the dismembered pieces into a frying pan along with some handfuls of snow and slammed it atop the stove. "If we can't roast the damn thing we'll *stew* it!" he exploded.

"Thash a damn good idea," lisped Slim. "Let's all get stewed along with the ruddy turkey."

"Wop's" culinary activities were interrupted by Flynn Harris, whose unerring nose for liquor had led him to the spot. "Did I ever tell you," he inquired with a diabolical leer, "how I came to leave the Hudson's Bay?"

"No!" "Wop" growled.

"It was when I was Inspector," Flynn chuckled, fixing one eye on "Wop" and another on a distant part of the room. "Got lubricated aboard the old *Grahame* at Fort Chipewyan after promising Chief Factor Fughl I'd stay on the wagon. Guess I fell overboard a couple of times, along with the bills of lading, and Fughl got sore and fired me." He puffed vigorously on his malodorous short, cutty-pipe. "So, I grabbed my blanket . . . paddled ashore, and slept it off on the rocks.

Next morning," Flynn chuckled malevolently, "I was there but—the steamer wasn't. So I cut wood all winter, then landed this job as Magistrate and Indian Agent through the Bishop, bless his soul."

"Come and get it!" yelled Walter, ladling a chunk of boiled turkey from the pan, "and look for your names on the place cards!"

With the improvised table too small for anything but the grub, each grabbed a tin plate, enamel mug and knife and fork, squatted on the nearest packing case or bedroll and proceeded to make the most of the Christmas feast of boiled turkey *sans* trimmings, leathery bannock smeared with butter melted to the consistency of train-oil, and cake frozen in the centre though decidedly gooey on the outside.

"Wop" sank his teeth determinedly into a rubbery drumstick. "This," his frost-bitten face crinkled into a wry grin, "is what is known in polite society as a 'buffet supper' so hop to it and help yourselves. But don't forget," he forced one of Flynn's swivel eyes to meet his own, "that this is the *last* of the Old Buck rum!"

What that Christmas dinner in that frost-bound cabin in the heart of the primeval wilderness lacked in fancy frills and trimmings was more than made up for in noisy joviality and heart-warming Northern camaraderie. Not till the small hours of the morning did the *mukluk*-shod guests weave their way homeward through the ghostly phosphorescence of the flickering *aurora*, their ears assailed by cannon-like reports as trees burst asunder from the bitter cold. "Wop" and his pilots sank wearily into their eiderdowns on the pole floor, oblivious to the wavering strains of Slim's alcoholic tenor who shattered the silvery silence with the last verse of *The Song of the North:*

An' some mor-r-n at half-pash two, when I crawl in my—hic—igloo
After sitting wiv a frien' who wash in pain.
She'll be waitin' for me there wiv the ham-bone of a bear,
An' she'll swat me when the Ice Worms nest again.

Note: During the writer's earlier years in the North—at Trout Lake Post near Hudson Bay—*only two mails a year were received*, one in the spring by an Indian packet-man, and another in summer by coast boat and York boat from York Factory. This also applied at other posts in the North at that time. By comparison the frequent air-borne mail of the present age is all the more striking.—P.H.G.

9

LAND OF THE NUNATAGMUITS

Soaring again into the frigid sky, the flight from the old-fashioned trading post of Fort Good Hope to Arctic Red River, with its heterogeneous collection of sprawling log huts and odoriferous fish-stages, was without incident. From there to Fort McPherson and Aklavic, the last day's hop assumed very much the air of a joy-ride. With the short distance—and the end of the 1,800 mile trail in sight—the take-off was accomplished into a sky diffused with the blood-red glow of the hidden sun, which stubbornly refused to climb up over the horizon from its winter hibernation.

The jump across the portage from Arctic Red River to Fort McPherson, though a hard day's trip by dog-team, was covered in a short twenty minutes by "Wop" and Glyn Roberts, while some thirty-five frozen lakes in as many miles allayed any fear of trouble in event of a forced landing. Down below, winding through a maze of white-frosted willows, the Rat River weaved its tortuous way from La Pierre House, overland summer route to the heart of the Yukon and Alaska. Little did the pilot of the *Lady Edmonton* realize at that moment how Fate was to link him, a couple of years later, with this region. Of how that busy weaver was to set the stage here for still another Arctic tragedy, and cast him in one of the leading roles.

From 3,000 feet (wrote Frederick Watt) the sun itself was almost in view, its reflection stretching along the skyline like a great red-hot wire and tinting the clouds with soft shades of rose. Ahead the upper vertebrae of the continent's backbone rose in rugged beauty with a continuous line of snow-capped peaks and purple-shadowed valleys. Fort McPherson, another huddle of log cabins, came in sight directly ahead. It was a tribute to May's navigation in view of the fact that he was going over the ground for the first time. The flagship dipped immediately to the Peel River which flows before the fort situated atop a high yellow cutbank a hundred yards back from the shore.

The *Mills*, keeping to the air, acknowledged the raising of the red ensign with the magic letters "H.B.C." with a series of aerial curtsies. John Melvin, Hudson's Bay Inspector, and a passenger from Fort Good Hope were set ashore with mail for the post. Without loss of time the *Lady Edmonton* again arose and the noses of the two ships were pointed across the immense network of the Mackenzie Delta straight towards the nearby Polar Sea and Aklavic and the achievement of more than two weeks' frigid effort.

Forty-five minutes later, the *Lady Edmonton* and the *Mills* swept down before the unimpressive settlement of Aklavic, in the land of the genial Nunatagmuits, to receive an enthusiastic reception from a cosmopolitan crowd of traders, Mounted Police, missionaries, and tall, smiling Nunatagmuit Eskimos gay in white mountain-goat-skin and hairy caribou-skin *parkas*, brilliantly embroidered *mukluks*, and huge polar bear-skin mittens slung from their necks by betasseled cords of worsted. As at every post from Fort Chipewyan down, the huskies immediately raised their pointed snouts to the skies and gave vent to their own wolfish and spine-chilling paeans of welcome. The landing before the semi-circular shore—crowned with a scattering of log huts, and the frame buildings of the Mounted Police, the Royal Signal Corps and Anglican Mission—marked the termination of what Walter Hale insisted was "a truly historical flight," and saw the last of the five tons of mail that had cluttered up the post office at the end-of-steel delivered to its destination.

No sooner had the planes landed than Bishop Geddes, attired in a magnificent wolverine-trimmed *parka* and blue-and-red *mukluks*, drove up with a team of wire-haired huskies. As Aklavic's official postmaster, he proceeded to ferry the precious cargo of mail ashore to where an eager group of exiles awaited in anxious anticipation to lend a hand in "sorting" it—which merely meant each one grabbed his own mail and discarded everything else!

Here, Northern hospitality in its warmest form descended upon the fliers, completely breaking up the party. May and Sims were whisked off to the Roman Catholic Mission; Walter Hale to the home of Bishop Geddes; Van der Linden was appropriated by Sergeant Hersey and the Wireless boys; Glyn Roberts by genial Dr. Urquhart, the Government

Agent, while Frederick Watt was taken under the wing of Corporal Fielding of the Mounted Police, all of which presaged a three-day round of friendly feasting, Eskimo dances and entertainment *à la mode*, nothing being spared to make the welcome as convivial and as lavish as possible. Not satisfied with merely making every hour of their stay one of heart-warming pleasure, the delighted exiles at this Arctic outpost showered their guests with gifts of all kinds. Handsome *parkas* and *mukluks* were presented to nearly every member of this historic flight, while May and Hale fell heir to dazzling white polar bear-skins as souvenirs of their Arctic visit.

When not up to his ears in a mountain of mail, Walter Hale permitted his inquiring mind to gather a mass of colourful and interesting information on the background of Aklavic and the genial Nunatagmuit Eskimos, all of whom were in to the post with their dog-teams and families to participate, in their own whole-hearted way, in everything pertaining to the white *Kablunats'* Christmas.

His unerring instinct led him to the snow-drifted abode of "Cogmollock Pete" Peterson. A hard-bitten old salt who resembled an old-time pirate with the red bandana wound around his head and huge, gold ear-rings dangling from his frost-bitten cauliflower ears, he had sailed the seven seas and landed in the Arctic, to bunk-up with a Cogmollock woman, conveniently forgetting his legal spouse in distant Sweden until forcibly reminded of her existence by the Swedish Consul in Edmonton. While Pete chewed snooce contentedly in his babiche-netted throne, the lady of the house—a veritable mountain of flesh enveloped in an immense, shapeless Mother Hubbard of green, yellow and scarlet bed-ticking, squatted on the floor, dutifully chewing the soles of her lord and master's sealskin *mukluks* to soften them.

In a sonorous mingling of Swedish and broken English, Pete delved into the past and gave his version of the measures used in moulding the primitive Eskimos into the requirements of Caucasian commerce. He told how, thanks to the ruthlessness of whalers and traders, the indiscriminate sale of whiskey, shoddy clothes and firearms, and the introduction of syphilis, measles and other white man's diseases, the once healthy Eskimos of the Delta had been reduced, in a few short years, from two thousand to fifty—though this number had been eventually increased to some four hundred by additions from the Baillie Island natives to the eastward. It was a sordid story of exploitation and greed, and only the fortuitous arrival of the Mounted Police at Herschel Island had saved the natives from annihilation. As it was, he continued, the Eskimos had been encouraged to destroy the once mighty herds of caribou by the indiscriminate sale of high-powered rifles and limitless supplies of ammunition until at last they had been converted from hunters into *trappers,* and reduced to dependence on the white man's trading post—and credit—which was of little avail in poor fur years, or when the fur market took a nose-dive.

Walter's face was serious as he strode back to the Bishop's house. Unquestionably here, as elsewhere in the North, was a grave and expensive native problem in the making!

Since his school days, when Inspector Denny LaNauze had reached Edmonton with the Eskimo slayers of Fathers Rouvier and LeRoux, "Wop" had always had a soft spot in his heart for these simple people of the polar spaces. Now he seized the opportunity to get acquainted with the tall, smiling Nunatagmuits who herded around, begging him to take them up and offering white fox and other pelts in payment. His plane overhauled, he took them aloft, six at a time. Like children, they roared vociferous appreciation, a guttural shouting and yelling emanating from the cockpit all the time they were in the air. None of them seemed the least bit afraid. In fact, they would have remained all day in the air had they suited their own inclinations.

"Gorman and I sure missed the boat!" grinned the delighted May as he finally grounded the plane. "We should have done our barnstorming down here instead of on the prairies." He gestured towards a laughing group of Huskies still waving furs in his face and pointing to the sky. "We sure would have made a clean-up!"

"How much for you sell 'um?" gravely inquired one of his latest passengers.

"What would you do with it?" "Wop" laughed, realizing the suggestion was offered in all seriousness.

"*You* fly 'im! *I* fly 'im!"

The prompt answer depicted the Eskimo's unwavering confidence in the equality, and superiority of his race over that of the white *Kablunat*. If a white man could fly a "mechanical bird" then—why not an Eskimo?

Before they left Aklavic, "Wop" and Walter Hale had ample opportunities to appreciate the mechanical ability and skill of these far from simple people. Every worthwhile Nunatagmuit, they learned, owned a two-masted schooner, in which he made his home during the summer—and hauled out before the freeze-up, all of the vessels having been brought in from Edmonton, Seattle or Vancouver and sold for the equivalent of five thousand dollars in white fox pelts, the aggregate value of the Eskimo fleet—scattered to all points of the compass during the winter, but sure to converge on Aklavic after open water—approximating a quarter of a million dollars. Winchester rifles and gramophones had been amongst their earlier white acquisitions. Now, most of the Eskimo ladies owned washing machines and sewing machines; two of the oldest patriarchs actually possessed Corona *type-writers*, while old Pokiak, the medicine man, had installed a Delco lighting plant in his log "igloo" where he delighted to amaze the less sophisticated Eskimos by making the "moon" flood the interior with its radiance at the magic touch of a switch. Poor Walter had nearly dropped with amazement when a smiling Eskimo youngster in skin clothing had politely asked him to pose while he snapped his camera!

From the time the fliers arrived in Aklavic till their departure for the south just before noon on December 30th there had not been a dull moment. Every night saw some affair in honour of the Commercial Airways fleet. On Friday it was an Eskimo dance, when some three hundred Nunatagmuits gave exhibitions of the Eskimo interpretation of the *Hula-Hula*, or went through the mummery of hunting seal and enemies to the accompaniment of immense tambourine-shaped polar bear-gut drums. On Saturday it was a caribou dinner with Bishop Geddes and his charming wife. On Monday night Sergeant Hersey of the Wireless Corps introduced them to a succulent mountain-sheep feast while, between times, "Wop" and Glyn Roberts became frequent visitors at the home of Inspector A. N. Eames of the Mounted Police who had replaced the veteran Stuart T. Wood the year before, and was still a little new to the Arctic and its ways.

A forty-below zero temperature, driven home by a brisk wind, failed to prevent the settlement of Aklavic from turning out *en masse*, despite blue noses and frost-bitten ears, to wish "Wop" and his cohorts Godspeed on their southern trek back to the end-of-steel. Bishop Geddes and his *parka*-clad wife boarded the flagship along with Joe Greenland, a half-breed trapper who had sent his dog-team ahead to Fort McPherson to make certain that, at the last moment, he would not forsake his determination to follow his first air-trail. The centre of a group of admiring Loucheux Indians prior to the take-off, he proved game to the end when aloft, answering all inquiries as to whether he was enjoying himself with an unmistakable forced smile. Whenever "Wop" hit a bump his fur cap would rise a couple of inches from his forehead, whereupon he would yank it firmly back in place, grimly affirming that this was "great stuff." His "smile" changed to a wide grin of relief, however, when his moccasined feet finally came into contact with terra firma at the little fort on the Peel.

Low oil pressure caused a delay at Fort McPherson. So cold was it that several members of the party, including the chief pilot, suffered from frost bites, Mrs. Geddes, a trained nurse, being kept busy administering to the sufferers.

As at Aklavic, the lonely exiles surged out to greet the fliers, who had the opportunity of meeting the bearded veteran, John Firth, and his diminutive, dwarf-like Loucheux squaw. For over forty years old John, as Hudson's Bay factor, had been a sort of uncrowned king to the nomad Loucheux Indians and the Delta Eskimos, who had done all their trading at the little fort on the hill. Only once during this long exile in the Back of the Beyond had John Firth gone Outside. Headed for his old home in the far-off Orkney Islands, he had scuttled back from Winnipeg to this God-forsaken spot with the assertion that, after a few days, civilization became "too *damned* monotonous!"

The hop across the portage to Arctic Red River was speedily accomplished but here Sims and Van der Linden, reinforced by May, put in a far from pleasant evening correcting the flagship's defective oil pressure. In forty-five below weather, they were forced to work by the dubious light of a flickering lantern. It was one o'clock in the morning when they returned, half frozen, to the warmth of Factor R.W. Dodman's dwelling.

"The sight of them," Watt recalled, "as they emerged like a brace of snowmen into the light was a fit subject for an epic poem."

Just twenty-six days after heading north on the initial air-mail flight, "Wop" and his fellow fliers were back at the end-of-steel, prepared to head north again with the next consignment of mail. The return trip proved uneventful, the only features of special interest consisting of several varieties of wild game sighted when the planes were flying low. A splendid and unusually compact herd of buffalo were spotted on the reserve above Fort Fitzgerald, while moose and masses of migrating caribou were sighted in considerable numbers near Fort Chipewyan.

A nonchalant, retiring sort of chap met the party as they climbed the bank at Fort McMurray and wished them a Happy New Year. It was Harold Farrington of Western Canada Airways, whose Fokker had passed them fifty miles south of Fort Good Hope. It appeared that Harold had made a forced landing forty miles from Fort Simpson, due to gas shortage while carrying out Corporal Cummings of the Mounted Police on a mercy flight. Sustained by the bar of chocolate in his pocket, and a pair of snowshoes, Farrington mushed the forty miles in twenty-four hours, loaded some gas on a dog-sled, and finally brought his ship and passenger out. It would have been a tough trip even for an experienced Northerner with dogs, but for a man encased in a flying suit, and unaccustomed to snowshoe travel, it seemed well-nigh unbelievable to old-timers.

While the North was enjoying the advantages of the air-borne letters, magazines, newspapers and other hitherto unknown winter luxuries, Paul Trudel, Postmaster at Fort Smith, was having anything but a pleasant time. To the dusky ladies of the fur lands the air-mail seemed to carry an inestimable boon as each became possessed of a fat Mail Order catalogue upon the gaudy pages of which appeared, in bright and attractive colours, all the latest things that the much-envied white women were wearing to the southward. It did not take long for the convent-reared native girls to realize that here, at last, was the chance to fulfil their life's ambition to be as well dressed as the traders' wives. It seemed *so* simple! All you had to do was just fill in the Order Form, and, if you hadn't any money, you merely wrote down the letters "C.O.D." and left the rest to Fate. So, they filled out Order Forms galore—not only for themselves but for those who couldn't write— and sent them merrily on their way.

When the next air-mail arrived, Paul Trudel looked askance at the colossal mountain of parcels by which he was surrounded, each marked "C.O.D.", addressed to Dora Ratfat, Mary Rabbit-Lung, Elsie Lame Duck, Helen Dry Meat, Mrs. LaHache and many other fantastic- ally-named ladies of the Lone Land. Then, one by one, the smiling faces of these backwoods beauties appeared at the wicket.

When Paul patiently explained they couldn't get their parcels in *debt*—that this was no trading post—but had to pay cash on the spot their indignation knew no bounds. From house to house, and store to store, they paraded, begging plaintively for the loan of anywhere from ten to sixty dollars. They would scrub, they said; wash clothes, make moccasins—in fact, do almost *anything* at some distant and indefinite date—if they could *only* get the cash to obtain the coveted parcels from that "son-of-a-bitch Paul" who was withholding, without any justification, what was rightfully their own!

Most of the parcels went back, but another mountain of them came in on the next plane—and they were still coming in when the steamer arrived in the summer—and it was quite a while ere the Mail Order houses realized that the Mary Rabbit-Lungs and Elsie Lame Ducks weren't, despite their substantial orders, the type of customers they craved.

On May 1st, "Wop" was accorded the distinction of having per- formed "The most meritorious service for the advancement of Canadian Aviation during 1929" by the award of the McKee Trophy in acknowledgment of his mercy flights, and in climaxing his record the previous December with the delivery of the first Arctic air-mail to Aklavic, and the completion of the inaugural flight over the longest and most northerly mail route in the world.

The Edmonton *Journal*, vastly pleased with the award editorialized:

It is not so much the trophy, as what it stands for that sheds a particular lustre on the recipients. It is given to the flier who, in the previous year, did the most to advance aviation in the Dominion. This is a wide field indeed to cover. There have been many notable flights in the Dominion in the last two years, but the feat of Dickins in opening the Barren Lands to aerial navigation, for which "Punch" received the trophy last year, and the equally important work of May in mercy flights into isolated settlements in the north, and in establishing the air mail service to Aklavic stand out above all others.

1 0

THE
"BLACK-GANG"

A s W. Leigh Brintnell was flying Gilbert Labine around the southern shoreline of Great Bear Lake in the fall of 1929, the prospector, peering through the humming shrouds on his way back, surveyed the ground below with an expert eye. He had studied the geological reports of Charlie Camsell and Major MacIntosh Bell, the first whites to investigate the mineral possibilities of this lonely region since the days of Samuel Hearne, as well as those of George M. Douglas.

At Echo Bay—where the eyes of the world became focused later— he noted streaks of orange splashed across the lake shore. The significance of the sight impressed itself upon him. At all costs, he must get his hands upon a chunk of this stained rock! When, the following April, he again flew back to this region with his partner, F. C. St. Paul, he realized as the plane zoomed in a wide circle above the spot he pointed out that, in the excitement of the previous flight, he had failed to plot the site correctly. It was a wild and desolate country, this; of rock-ribbed ridges, bold crags and deeply scored canyons dotted with stunted spruce and finger-like rampikes—the No-Man's Land lying between the Eskimo territory and the hunting grounds of their ancestral enemies, the Indians. Finally, he pointed out a place to land and waved the air-pilot good-bye, only to discover that he had alighted on the wrong spot. Somewhere, probably covered deep beneath the snows which still blanketed the uncharted shores to the eastward, lay the place he sought.

Hacking out a couple of light, birch toboggans, and loading them with what they needed, the two prospectors slipped on their snowshoes and tramped across the glaring drifts, almost blinded by the dazzling brilliance of the spring sun on the burnished surface. A blizzard of fierce impetuosity burst upon them, buffeting them about, and whipping the snow into their eyes. Before it was spent, St. Paul was snow-blind and unable to carry on. Making camp in the protection of some dwarf spruce and cutting plenty of firewood, Labine left his partner there and carried on alone. At last there seemed to be something vaguely familiar about his surroundings but he could not be sure since the country, from the air, presented an entirely different aspect to what it did from the ground. Yet the points, the ridges, the contours of the shoreline and the bays, gradually took on the picture that had burned itself into his brain through months of anxious waiting. Within a few hours he was back in camp, carrying in his hand a piece of the coveted rock with the yellow stain.

When the plane returned, he flew a thousand miles south from Echo Bay to Edmonton with rock specimens in his dunnage-bag. Quickly, the rocks were despatched to Ottawa. There assayers crushed them, dissolved them in their retorts, tested the products with their delicate electroscopes, and submitted their report. Labine had made no mistake! He had discovered pitchblende—the mother-lode of radium—one of the most rare and valuable substances in the world. At last, the key with which to unlock the Northland's hidden treasure chest had been found, thanks to the aid of the bush pilots!

By May, 1931, some 4,500 claims had been staked, and camps were springing up everywhere. The first comprised a scattering of tents, and beds consisting of ice-covered boughs slashed from the stunted conifers. Firewood, owing to the proximity of the Barrens, was as scarce as hen's teeth, and the wet spruce so full of sap that it scarcely afforded enough heat for its own slow and spluttering combustion. Each morning, shivering men climbed from rabbitskin robes or sleeping-bags and painfully separated their beards from the bedding, to which they had congealed from their frozen breath. In the absence of draft animals, logs had to be hauled by sheer manpower for long distances over heavy snow, rugged chasms and steep hillsides, while daylight was so short that, for eighteen out of the twenty-four hours, they had to resort to the dim, smoky light of coal-oil lamps.

Yet, the thriving mining town of Eldorado continued, from such inauspicious beginnings, to go ahead with leaps and bounds until it was able to boast such modern conveniences as running water, electric light, a radio station, and regular air-mail and freight-passenger air service linking it with the Outside. Since transportation costs amounted to the almost incredible figure of $1.50 per pound, only the most indispensable articles were flown in as flour, at $150.00 a sack, became, literally, almost worth its weight in gold. From the days when

Sir John Franklin had wintered with Richardson and Back at Fort Franklin, on the south-west shore of this immense, eleven-thousand square mile lake with its rugged shores back in 1825, Great Bear Lake had been noted for its sterility. To add to the difficulties of pioneering, little game was to be found save the odd snowshoe rabbit or ptarmigan. Even the lake trout, known to frequent these frigid waters, seemed loathe to visit the nets so laboriously set through holes chiselled through six-feet or more of solid ice.

From its inception, the new settlement had been forced to depend entirely upon the aeroplane and the bush pilots for both transportation and supplies, since the only link with the Mackenzie River was by the shallow-and-swift-flowing Bear River, broken by a series of bad rapids. Eventually, through the capable management of the veteran bush-pilot, Matt Berry, and Raoul Bertrand, a Toronto mining man, these difficulties were overcome to some extent with the installation of Diesel-engined tugs and barges operating above and below a portage road around the Bear River Rapids. But, for passengers, mail, and light freight, the aeroplane continued to be the lifeline linking Eldorado with the great Outside.

Bush-flying being still in its infancy, and radio communication with the North still but a shadow of its present self, when an airplane left the railhead on any of these long northern flights it simply disappeared into the frosty ether for days on end, and the only assurance of its welfare was when it reappeared at its base once more. Though this made for greater hazards than exist today, owing to the impossibility of securing weather reports, or aid in case of trouble, it encouraged extreme care and resourcefulness on the part of the pilot, who realized that, once away from his base, the lives of everybody concerned depended solely upon his wisdom and judgment. There could be no possible *second* chance in case of faulty judgment—which is probably one of the reasons why those early years of bush-flying developed so many outstanding Canadian bush-pilots.

Throughout the history of bush-flying the pilot has invariably captured the spotlight. As a consequence, the general impression has been that the pilot of a plane engaged in some outstanding flight should be given all the credit. As a matter of fact, any experienced pilot will tell you that, while appreciating this tribute to himself, he owes a debt of deep gratitude to the courage of the mechanics through whose unselfish courage and co-operation in facing hardships and meeting emergencies the North has been relatively free from major accidents. Very seldom in newspaper or other reports is the mechanic ever mentioned yet, in all outstanding flights, some quietly efficient mechanic in greasy overalls has usually been riding beside the pilot, sharing all the difficulties and hardships of the trip for far less remuneration—and infinitely less recognition—than is accorded to the man at the controls.

Northern bush-flying is essentially a two-man job. If such were not the case aviation companies would be quick to sacrifice the mechanic's weight for so much extra pay-load, since every pound of unnecessary weight is carefully eliminated in aerial transportation. Not only is the mechanic's presence necessary but his contribution to the joint teamwork is usually of the most unpleasant and exacting kind. Exposed to the elements at temperatures often as low as sixty-below zero, he is forced to work with bare hands, handling freezing metal, since it is impossible to undertake such repairs wearing clumsy gloves or mittens. Nevertheless, repairs must be undertaken promptly, regardless of biting cold and slashing, knife-edged winds. Furthermore, despite the fact that the mechanic's ungloved fingers are seared constantly with frost-bite, he is unable to warm them since it would be unsafe to have a fire nearby, or even to bring a blow-torch in close proximity to the inflammable structure of the plane. So, he grits his teeth and carries on until the job is done—and considers it all part of the day's work!

Frequently, during the frigid winter weather, the fabric of the underbody of the plane is pierced by jagged up-thrusts of ice. To effect the necessary repairs the jagged edges of the cut must be sewn together with heavy linen thread and patched. This necessitates the mechanic lying flat on his back on rough ice, with his neck arched at an angle that is the last word in refined torture. In the summertime, a mechanic repairing a damaged pontoon may be immersed to his waist in frigid Arctic water while the rest of his body is exposed to the torment of myriads of mosquitoes, "bull-dogs" and blackflies, unable to fend them off since his hands are fully occupied with repair work.

As a matter of fact, every aircraft leaving its base is supposed to be fully equipped and self-sustaining for at least a couple of weeks in case of a crash. If the craft makes a forced landing upon some nameless lake, or in the heart of the Barrens, the crew are expected not only to take care of themselves but to look after the passengers as well. Consequently, each plane carries emergency equipment comprising, amongst other things, an eiderdown sleeping-bag for each of the crew, a silk tent and a light tin stove with collapsible stovepipes; concentrated food; snow-shovels, first-aid kit, rifle and ammunition; fishing gear, large plumbers' firepots for heating the engine after overnight stops, and oil-pails to hold the engine oil—which must be drained every night in the cold weather and re-heated next morning.

Sammy Tomlinson, Lou Parmenter, Bill Nadin and other air-engineers who serviced these Northern planes when bush-flying was in its infancy knew what it was like to crawl protestingly from an eiderdown robe on the floor of some trading post two hours before the first exploratory shafts of dawn lighted the star-filled sky, hastily kindle a fire to ward off the bitter cold and complete the process of donning winter clothing, seldom more than partially removed, then trudge across the rough *bordeaux* and up-ended ice of the Mackenzie before breakfast in fifty-below weather, sometimes blinded by a bitter nor'-wester carrying swirling curtains of stinging snow before it, then suck hundreds of cubic feet of carbon monoxide into their innards on an empty stomach ere warming up the engine of a frozen plane with a blow-torch. Many a day's work was started on what the mechanics called "a Hudson's Bay breakfast"—a belly-full of wind and a drink of cold water. In those days, when bush-flying was really tough, their only hangar was a storm-tossed piece of tarpaulin.

Aided by the rays of the indispensable flashlight—which shared his bed so that the battery wouldn't freeze—the mechanic would light the two heating-torches and, fire extinguisher in hand, disappear under the tarp. Having picked up the two heavy pails of engine-oil, he would make for a spot in the shelter of some rocks, or bush, where he had already dug a hole in the snow and kindled a fire. For an hour, half-smothered in the increasing fumes of carbon monoxide in his cramped quarters beneath his tattered "hangar," he would watch with an alert eye the heating of the engine lest an unnoticed drop of oil should cause a fire which could, in a few minutes, transform the plane into a blazing furnace. When the oil was ready, and the engine brought to summer temperature, the oil would be quickly poured into the tanks, the gasoline valves turned on, and the canvas removed. Then, before the Arctic cold had time to chill the engine, the self-starter was brought into use and the motor would burst into a staccato roar that would echo back from the wall of snow-mushroomed evergreens. Once started, it would be revved up until engine and oil had been heated to running temperature.

In the meantime, the engineer would have carefully inspected the wing surfaces for signs of hoar-frost which might not only result in a loss of "lift" but in sudden disaster. When the snow was cleared from around the skis, the passengers' baggage stored, the engineer would signal the pilot. Shutting off the engine only long enough to permit the passengers to hustle aboard, he would taxi his plane along its snowy runway and roar off into the frigid skies.

"A day's work done," to quote Walter Gilbert, "before the city dweller first blinks a dubious eye—such is the typical beginning of an Arctic flying day in winter!"

From the moment of the take-off, until the empurpled shadows of coming night enfolded the spectral pines in their dark mantle, the engine seldom stopped since even a short halt might chill it and the oil-tanks to a point that might make re-starting impossible, and necessitate the repetition of the early morning's arduous work.

All day the business of flying kept the crew steadily on their toes. When stops were close the frequent rustling of cargo, with the eternal struggle to break-out the heavy steel drums of gasoline from frozen snowbanks, kept the crew on the go. So little time was there to spare that seldom did they enjoy the luxury of a hot lunch at mid-day. Instead, they wolfed down a sandwich after it was hurriedly thawed over the pilot's cockpit heater.

Since Northern flying has now given way to scheduled operations, and mechanical aids are available all along the routes, the erstwhile team of pilot and mechanic who worked, slept and ate together for weeks at a time, is fast becoming a thing of the past—and will soon be but a memory.

As "Wop" continued to establish new records in flying mail twixt the end-of-steel and the Arctic he found in the free and easy *camaraderie* of the North something that recalled those Air Force days in France though, here, there was an intangible something that was more appealing. A Northern friendship disregarded all barriers of rank and social status, and was given wholeheartedly and not for favours to come. It was a friendship of shared hardships, dangers and loneliness. Profiting by the mistakes of one or two of the earlier airmen, "Wop" wisely refused to be drawn into any of the bitter fur trade feuds which—originating in the fierce jealousy and competition of opposition traders, and conflicting personalities thrown into cramping proximity—rocked most of the forts and settlements to the core. Firmness, tact, and a knowledge of human psychology learned by bitter experience overseas caused him to adopt this wise course and thus avoid the pitfalls of some of his predecessors.

The latter part of 1931 witnessed far-reaching changes in the organization of the major companies operating down the Mackenzie River. In August, Western Canada Airways absorbed a number of small Eastern companies which were experiencing difficulties as a consequence of the great Depression entwining its octopus-like tentacles about every commercial enterprise in the land. Expanding its rapidly-increasing services from the Atlantic to the Pacific, and taking over Commercial Airways, along with the Bellancas and the mail contract, it changed its name to Canadian Airways, Limited. Thenceforth, "Wop" May's red Bellanca bore the insignia of the grey goose, and he found himself rubbing shoulders, in an intimacy born of new associations, with Walter Gilbert, Pilot Mullen, and engineers Bowen, Hardman, Heuss, King and Parmenter, with "Punch" Dickins installed as Superintendent of Western Lines in Edmonton.

Thanks to the aerial stampedes to Great Bear Lake, precipitated by

Gilbert Labine and D'Arcy Arden, Canadian Airways and other companies were transporting supplies into the interior in a dozen or more machines as compared with the two lone planes that ventured in in 1929, while Bill Jewitt, the "flying prospector," nonchalantly commuted between his Great Bear Lake holdings and Edmonton in his private Moth—a distance of a thousand miles!

In July, Charles Lindberg and his *petite* and charming wife had flown to the Orient by way of Ottawa, Moose Factory, Fort Churchill; across the Barren Lands to Aklavic, thence to Point Barrow and Nome, thereby giving a further boost to the possibilities of Arctic air travel, and to short-cuts across the roof of the world to Asia and Europe.

While flying was still considered a hazardous enterprise to the southward, the airplane had already, thanks to the resourcefulness and ability of the bush-pilots, become a commonplace factor in the life of the Far North along with the canoe and the dog-team.

Meanwhile, events were shaping up that were to display the airplane and the bush-pilot in still another of their many phases of originality and usefulness.

11

THE MAD TRAPPER
OF RAT RIVER

I t was July, 1931, and Fort McPherson lay somnolent and languid under the tropic heat of the short Arctic summer, the balmy air pulsating with the drowsy drone of myriads of mosquitoes, and the distant booming of a Loucheux tom-tom.

Squatted on the floor of the trading store were a number of belated Loucheux hunters waiting their turn to barter their lynx and bear skins with beetle-browed William Firth, the factor. His stiff-brimmed Stetson pushed back on his head, Constable "Spike" E. Millen of the Mounted Police leaned on the unpainted counter chatting with the grey-bearded veteran, John Firth, and cursing the luck that had transferred him from Cambridge Bay in the land of the Cogmollocks to the uneventful daily round at Arctic Red River, a few miles to the southward.

Not a soul around that little trading post had the faintest inkling that, a short distance to the westward, there was being enacted the first of a series of incidents that were soon to lead to a dramatic climax and hold, spell-bound, not only the Northland but the entire Outside world as well. Neither did the three Loucheux bucks, whose coppery faces peered through the thickly-matted willows half a day's journey to the westward, realize that the lone occupant of the flimsy raft that had just swung around a bend of the serpentine Peel was going to have any particular influence on their lives. With photographic detail, their sharp black eyes observed that the man was wiry, slightly stoop-shouldered, had light brown hair and a slightly up-turned nose, and that he handled his craft like a veteran trapper. Suddenly, his ice-blue eyes encountered the dark visages of the red men.

"Hey! mahogany-face," came the surly demand. "Is this the Porcupine River?" No friendly smile lighted the predatory face of the stranger as his arrogant question floated across the water.

For a moment the Loucheux regarded him in disapproving silence.

"No!" snapped Indian Joe curtly. "Him Peel Ribber—him *not* Porcupine!"

"*Hell!*" snarled the stranger. With an angry thrust of his pole, he sent the raft leaping towards the bend ahead.

Three pairs of inscrutable eyes watched as it vanished among the willows then, with guttural grunts of contempt, the three hunters turned their moccasined feet towards the fort. Already they cherished in their hearts an Indian hatred for the surly stranger—a hatred that, later, was to blaze into fierce intensity.

A couple of weeks slipped by. Constable Millen gazed disconsolately through the windows of the Arctic Red River barracks across the billowing mass of rank greenery at the tumble-down shacks and odoriferous fish-stages that made up this unattractive settlement. Above the drone of mosquitoes came the staccato exhaust of a motor and into the muddy landing chugged an Eskimo schooner from Aklavic. As Millen reached the river-bank a grinning Nunatagmuit in a white dickey handed him a confidential memo from Inspector Eames dated Aklavic, July 12th:

It is reported that a strange white man, going by the name of Johnson, landed near Fort McPherson on July 9th. Apparently he came down-river on a raft, tying up below the settlement and walking into the post . . . He had neither outfit, rifle nor dogs, but appeared to be amply supplied with money. Please make inquiries in the district and submit a report, but do not make a special patrol.

A hurried visit to Fort McPherson elicited the information that Albert Johnson carried a large sum of money, in big bills, tucked away in small, tight rolls in every pocket. Though surly to a degree, and angrily resenting any questions concerning himself, he had given no trouble.

"He comes in and gets what he wants," William Firth told Millen. "Pays for it, and bothers no one. Says he wasn't staying in the district so we didn't need to know all about him!"

Anxious to size up this Johnson for himself, Millen at last succeeded in crossing his trail. The meeting occurred at Fort McPherson as Johnson was packing supplies down to his canoe. "Good-day!" "Spike" greeted him affably and stopped. "What's your name?" he asked, his voice friendly and unconcerned. "I don't seem to have seen your face around here before!"

"Albert Johnson!" came the surly answer. "Who in hell wants to know?"

"Where do you come from?"

"Arctic Red River!"

Millen eyed the so-called Johnson keenly. "You *don't* come from Arctic Red River," he stated bluntly. "That's my detachment—and I know everyone in the district." His eyes bored challengingly into the others. "Where are you from?" he reiterated quietly.

"Came down the Mackenzie from the prairie," Johnson growled with obvious resentment.

Again the man was lying! For a second Millen met that defiant, icy stare. "Where are you bound for?" he demanded.

"None of your *damned* business!" Johnson spat viciously. "I don't want nuthin' to do with the Police. There's allus trouble when they're aroun'!"

Turning contemptuously on his moccasined heel, he strode down the sandy trail towards the willow flats.

Standing there, tall and erect, on the brink of the precipitous bank, Constable Millen watched the receding form with a peculiar sense of foreboding.

"I'm afraid," he told William Firth when he entered the store, "that bird's going to give us trouble yet!" A remark that was to be vividly recalled a few months later.

On his mail flights to Aklavic, "Wop," too, heard from Eames and Riddell of the unwanted trapper, who had taken up his abode on the Rat River to the discomfiture of the local Indians, but, like the rest of the whites there, he didn't give the matter a further thought. All kinds of people found their way into the Silent Places and, if you're wise, you didn't ask any questions but took them for what they were—and simply left them alone.

Once again winter clamped down on the Northland, freezing solid the creeks and pools and the many-channelled delta of the Mackenzie and burying the frosted willows deep in driven snow. Loucheux hunters commenced to follow the fur trail on their webbed snowshoes, setting traps and deadfalls. Dog-teams shuttled back and forth with jingling bells between Arctic Red River, Fort McPherson and Aklavic. Fur-clad Mounties, urging their slant-eyed dogs along the forest trails, had almost forgotten the bushed trapper who, for a while, had made himself obnoxious along the winding Peel.

Christmas day found the genial and popular "Spike" Millen and Constable King the centre of a boisterous group of *parka*-clad trappers and traders in the snug log barracks at Arctic Red River. As evening closed down the celebration at the barracks took a more riotous and noisy turn. Suddenly the door swung open, admitting a billowing cloud of white vapour which almost obscured the hooded figure with frost-scarred face and whitened eyebrows.

"Dat white man!" the Loucheux snarled, his face creasing into lines of anger. "Him come from Yukon las' summer—now him pull'um up my traps an' hang 'em up in tree. His say *him* trapline ... Injun no trap dere!"

In quick, excited gutturals, the Indian poured out his story. A strange white man occupying a cabin on the Rat River had been terrorizing the Indians until they were afraid to hunt or trap. Now they were starving—with no furs with which to buy supplies and ammunition!

Millen turned to Constable King. "That bird Johnson again!" he growled as he gazed through the frosted panes at the blizzard that howled without. "Hate like hell to ask you to buck weather like this, but there's only one thing for it. Check up on this bird, and see if he's got a trapping license. If he hasn't he's no business trapping here at all. Guess you'll have to hit it with Joe Bernard in the morning!"

Late on the bitterly cold winter night of the 28th, Constable King and Joe Bernard trudged through a spume of snow and halted their dog-team before the Johnson cabin. Squat, ugly and forbidding— built of unusually heavy logs loop-holed at the corners—it stood in a snow-filled clearing on the north bank of the Rat, twenty miles from its junction with the Husky, and resembled an old-time frontier fort, or blockhouse, rather than a trapper's cabin.

"*Some* shack!" muttered King as he pounded with mittened fist upon the massive door. "Hey! open up," he shouted, his words whipped from his lips by the knife-edged wind.

Only dull echoes answered his summons. Ploughing around the cabin on his snowshoes, King observed that there were no tracks in the freshly-fallen snow to indicate that the trapper had left the place since the storm commenced.

Again he pounded the door. "Open up!" he shouted. "I know you're in there!" There was no response.

King shrugged his shoulders. "Guess we'll have to hit over to Aklavic," he told Bernard. "Can't do anything more without a warrant." With mounting anger, he again pounded on the door until it leapt and reverberated beneath his blows. Finally he picked up the head-line of his toboggan. "Come on," he snapped. "We might as well get going!"

In the moon-twilight of New Year's eve the police party appeared again before the cabin on the Rat. This time it comprised Constable King, Constable R. C. McDowell, and Lazarus Sitchinilli, one of the Loucheux headmen. All were armed with rifles and firearms while, in the pocket of his furred *ahtegi*, King carried a warrant empowering him to enter and search the trapper's dwelling.

With McDowell beside him, King pounded on the door. Silence! "Open in the name of the King!" came the demand. No answer! "OPEN—or we'll smash the door in!" King lifted an axe above his head.

BANG! Thunderous reverberations within the cabin accompanied the spiteful crack of the rifle. Splinters leapt outward as a bullet ripped through the door, sending King reeling, his body pierced by the leaden ball. Whipping out his revolver, McDowell poured a stream of fire through a loop-hole to draw attention from King as he crawled painfully towards the bush, leaving ominous stains upon the snow. With blazing guns pouring a shower of lead from the cabin's loop-holes, Sitchinilli crawled to where King lay—stunned and bleeding.

Braving the flaming guns, McDowell rushed to the side of his stricken comrade to find a growing stain on his *ahtegi* from a bullet hole beneath the heart. For a second he stood, horrified at the realization that eighty miles of the hardest kind of slogging lay between his dangerously wounded companion and the nearest doctor, at Aklavic—and the dogs dead tired! Defying, again the rifle of the mad-

150

man in the cabin, expecting each second to feel the bite of hot lead, he slung King over his shoulder and carried him to the safety of the river-bank. There he lashed him to the sled, picked up his whip and urged the dogs on towards Aklavic.

Twenty hours after his departure from the mad trapper's cabin, McDowell drove up to the Mission Hospital, at Aklavic and delivered King to the care of Dr. Urquhart, the record journey having been made without a single stop to make a fire, and with dogs that were thoroughly exhausted even at the outset!

Aklavic was thrown into a turmoil when news of the vicious shooting got around. *Parka*-clad men rushed to the barracks, rifle in hand, to offer help.

To Inspector Eames, the situation now stood out in all its stark reality. Johnson had committed a serious crime, a crime that was a direct challenge not only to himself but to the authority of the entire Force. Promptly, he snatched up the gauntlet. Through the frigid ether crackled a call from UZK—"The Voice of the Northern Lights"—calling all trappers throughout the Delta to join the police in hunting down the mad-dog, Johnson. Improvised by Quarter-master Sergeant Riddell and the boys of the Royal Canadian Corps of Signals for the entertainment of lonely trappers, this amateur broadcasting station was now to serve a vastly different purpose.

Mounted Police from Arctic Red River and Fort McPherson were ordered in to Aklavic for duty. Ere long, Inspector Eames surveyed his determined and grim-faced posse—a picturesque assemblage in their decorated snow-shirts, furred *ahtegis* and gaudy Eskimo *mukluks*. It comprised Constables Millen and McDowell, a couple of dark-visaged Loucheux guides, and trappers Noel Verville, Knud Lang, Karl Garlund and Ernest Sutherland.

Their wolverine-trimmed hoods pulled over their heads as protection from the blizzard that whistled about their ears, the posse whipped up their huskies and fell into a long, swaying line. Eames had secured some dynamite, intending to convert it into bombs to blast his way into the cabin, and this, with dog-feed, grub and a supply of ammunition had been lashed upon the sleds.

One thing cheered them on their way. A report from Dr. Urquhart that, unless complications developed, King would recover—thanks to Constable McDowell! The explosive bullet had smashed two ribs just below the heart, ploughed through King's body and broken two more at the point of exit. Only his posture with uplifted axe had prevented the bullet from penetrating the heart.

At last, through a smother of driving flakes, they espied the sinister shape of the loop-holed cabin. Circling the building under cover, Eames posted his men at strategic points and shouted to Johnson to surrender. The reply was prompt and uncompromising! From the cabin came the whip-like crack of a rifle, a spear of flame leapt from a loop-hole, sending a bullet whining over his head.

From the police guns a crackling fusillade rattled against the log walls of the cabin.

"Come on, boys," shouted Eames. "We'll rush him and smash the door in!"

From the rifles of the trappers burst a covering fire of stabbing flame as McDowell and Millen zigzagged across the clearing and brought their rifle butts smashing down upon the door. Blazing guns flared in their faces, forcing them to streak for cover, with the door but partly demolished.

"I got a squint through the door," cried the amazed Millen as he turned to the posse. "The shack was full of smoke, but I saw where he'd dug away down into the ground. The place's double-walled all around. Trapper's cabin . . . *hell*, it's a damned fortress! The only way's to dynamite him out of there!"

While bombs were being prepared, the posse crouched behind the snow-covered bush for protection from the blizzard that continued to moan and scream about them. Eames had decided to delay the attack till dawn in the hope that they might catch Johnson napping. At four o'clock everything was ready. Silent and sinister, the cabin lay there— an ebony rectangle against the empurpled snow. The blizzard had subsided, and stars winked coldly in a sky now lighted with the ghostly phosphorescence of the *aurora*.

"All right!" Eames called softly. Rising from behind a twisted pine,

Verville heaved a dynamite bomb against the cabin door. A rending detonation rocked the ground and almost split their ear-drums. The cabin seemed, suddenly, to burst into a welter of blood-red flame as though it had exploded. For a split second the clearing glowed with scarlet light, which changed to ebony blackness as the posse leapt with flaming guns towards the cabin.

Lurching to the shattered door, Knud Lang peered through the acrid smoke that eddied and swirled within. Half-conscious from the tremendous detonation, Johnson lay, inert, upon the floor, his eyes staring wildly through the murk. Knud pointed his gun—hesitated, and dropped the muzzle. "*Hell!*" his voice came clearly to the others. "I can't shoot a man with his eyes open like that!"

An automatic spat flame and bullets through the doorway. Johnson had suddenly become galvanized into life! With the rest of the posse at his heels, Knud fled for his very life.

In the forbidding gloom and silence of the forest they prepared for another attack. Flares sizzled into flame, lighting the icy ridge with a ghostly incandescence which revealed a ragged hole blown in the cabin roof, and the ridge-pole pointed crazily towards the star-spangled sky. Revolver in hand, Eames and Garlund prepared for another sortie. A four-pound bomb of dynamite sailed through the air and fell with nice precision squarely in the doorway. With a shattering roar it exploded, emitting a mushroom of red and yellow flame, and filling the air with splintered wood. Eames and Garlund launched themselves across the clearing. Unhurt, Johnson unleashed another fusillade. Struck by a bullet, the electric torch leapt from Garlund's hand. Eames' hat shot high in the air. With bullets singing like wasps about their ears, they swung aside and leapt again for the protection of the timber.

With the dynamite gone, food and dog-feed almost exhausted, the cold becoming more intense, and the mad trapper still, apparently, unharmed, Eames held another council among the dark and sentinel pines.

"Let's tough it out," growled Verville. "It won't be any worse for us than it will be for him in there!"

But Eames, realizing the serious consequences that might ensue if they failed to capture the cabin, or renew depleted supplies, decided otherwise. "It isn't worth the chance," he warned. "We've got to hit for Aklavic. As it is, we're going to run short of grub and dog-feed."

Muttering silently amongst themselves, the posse turned towards the frozen river. A last look at Johnson's fortress showed them the blasted and fire-scarred wall, the gaping doorway, the shattered roof and the up-ended ridge-pole. It was Verville who voiced their feelings as he shook his fist at the cabin. "You win this time, guy," he bellowed, "but don't forget—we're coming *back!*"

Five days later Inspector Eames was leading another posse from Aklavic towards the fortified cabin of the mad trapper, their sleds heavy-laden with rations, dog-feed, ammunition, and some stink-bombs ingeniously devised by Staff-Sergeant Hersey of the Wireless Corps from outboard-motor cylinders, gunpowder and sulphur. The original posse had been augmented by the addition of Quartermaster Sergeant R. F. Riddell and Staff-Sergeant Hersey, who carried with them a portable wireless transmitter. Adding their strength to the posse were the three Indians whom Johnson had treated with such contempt and scant courtesy on the Peel. Good weather, and hard-packed drifts, made travelling easier and faster and, on the third day out, they espied again the cabin they had such good reason to remember.

"Well," shouted Verville grimly as they climbed the bank, "here we are again, guy. Watch out!"

As they circled the cabin warily they noticed that its appearance had not changed, and that no attempt had been made to either repair the splintered door or the shattered roof. "He's flown the coop!" snapped Garlund.

Fearful of treachery, they crawled cautiously forward towards the wrecked shack, their numbed fingers caressing the icy triggers of their rifles. At last they reached the door and peered within. Johnson was gone! He had completely disappeared.

In stunned amazement they gazed around the cabin. The floor had been dug three feet below ground level, while the double-logged walls had completely turned the bullets of the police. Lying at his loop-holes and firing at his attackers, Johnson had been practically invulnerable from rifle bullets. The cabin still reeked with the odour of gunpowder. The inside was in a state of havoc, littered with masses of debris: beans, flour and other provisions scattered by the force of the dynamite explosion. Beneath their *mukluks* crunched scores of empty cartridge shells.

"For God's sake, look at this!" cried Hersey.

Crowding forward, they observed a gaping cavity in the earth in one corner of the cabin.

"A tunnel!" Millen ejaculated. "So that's why our dynamite failed to drive him out. That son-of-a-gun was prepared for *anything.*"

Searching the hard-packed snow of the clearing for tracks that might indicate the direction of Johnson's flight, they came across a cunningly concealed cache of food supplies two hundred yards behind the cabin. Millen shook his head. "What kind of a trapper's this Johnson anyway?" he muttered. "Look at all the labour entailed in digging that tunnel and dug-out, and double-walling the cabin. And not a trap or a pelt or a stretcher anywhere around. Why—he wasn't trapping at all! Then, he hides his food cache two hundred yards from his cabin to give himself more work. The whole thing's doggone crazy. It just don't make any sense!"

With Johnson's flight, Inspector Eames now realized the immensity of the problem which confronted the police. The rough Rat River country, with its rugged mountains, its tangled undergrowth, its winding streams and glaciers, and its snow-filled ravines gave the fugitive a tremendous advantage. And, a man of Johnson's type—a deadly shot, a superlative woodsman, wiry and fearless to the last degree—could be depended upon to utilize these advantages to the utmost. Furthermore, the constant winds that lurked and whipped about the mountains would quickly obliterate his tracks. While the "Mad Trapper" travelled light the large police party would necessarily be burdened with heavy baggage and weighty dog-feed.

Leaving the five men in camp in a clump of spruce beside the Rat, Eames deposited the loads, hitched up his dogs and soon the crunch!

Men involved in manhunt for Albert Johnson, the "Mad Trapper," 1932. Left to right: Sergeant R.F. Riddell; Sergeant H.F. Hersey, Royal Canadian Signals Corps; Duncan Bowen, brother of "Wop" May's mechanic; Norman Hancock; Sergeant Major C. Neary; Jack Ethier, trapper; Wilfred Reid "Wop" May. *Glenbow Archives NA-1258-101*

crunch! of snowshoes faded in the distance as he headed back to Aklavic.

For "Spike" Millen and his party there followed days of incredible toil prowling the river trails, floundering through the soft snow of deep ravines, searching the frost-rimed willows, and bucking the piercing winds as they explored the icy summits and snow-filled canyons for the snowshoe tracks of the fugitive. But not a sign did they find of the elusive trapper. Johnson had succeeded in completely covering up his tracks!

Eleven days out from the base camp, where they had parted with Eames, they drove their tired dogs past the granite-walled mouth of the Barrier River and, a few hours later, entered the mouth of a frozen creek confined between towering walls of rock. "A tough place to run into Johnson," vouchsafed Verville, his grey eyes noting apprehensively the countless jagged rocks, which offered ideal concealment for a lurking foe. "We'd sure make one *lovely* target against the white snow of this creek-bed!"

At last the redness departed from the sky, leaving a tinge of violet that, in an hour or so, would be transformed into ebony blackness. Crawling out of the canyon, they commenced to portage a sweeping bend. Suddenly Garlund dropped on his knees and uttered a hoarse exclamation. Quivering with excitement, he pointed ahead. "Look!" he cried softly. "He's there!"

Crouching behind a V-shaped barricade of logs in a clump of spruce that rose from the high bank of the frozen creek, some four hundred yards across the snow-swept niggerhead, was the dark but unmistakable figure of a man!

"Wop" Takes Up the Trail

"That's him, all right!" Riddell scanned the distant figure through his glasses. "It's getting dark now. Shall we wait and tackle him in the morning?"

Crouched behind the snow-swept hog-back, their eyes glued on the distant figure, they made their plans in hoarse whispers. They would retreat to the cover of the creek behind them, camp for the night and tackle the mad trapper in the morning.

As soon as the unseen sun painted the peaks with lavender and scarlet they were on the trail again. Climbing to the hog-back, they crawled carefully from one bunch of frost-rimed willows to another, stalking the man behind the barricade. They were still three hundred yards from Johnson's ambush when the dark figure rose upright, plainly silhouetted against the blue-white drifts of the snow.

Swinging his rifle to his shoulder, Garlund took swift aim and pressed the trigger. A deafening detonation rolled back and forth among the peaks as Johnson threw up his arms and toppled backwards behind the breastwork. Leaping down the slope, they threw themselves behind some rocks and bushes. Not a sign came from the ambush.

"Think you got him?" panted Millen.

Garlund snuggled down behind the rock and nodded. "Believe I did, 'Spike'. It was a chance shot. But . . . he may be playing possum!"

Crouching in the biting cold behind the rocks and willows, the posse watched the barricade with hawk-like vigilance. Two frigid hours crawled by without a sign of life or movement, the cold biting with numbing intensity deeper and deeper into their vitals. At last, Millen turned to Riddell, his face blue with cold. "What do you say—shall we risk it?"

"All right," snapped Riddell. "But advance in open order. Dash from rock to rock—and *don't* expose yourselves!"

Their faces grim and determined, Millen, Verville and Garlund nodded. Zigzagging from rock to rock, they reached the bank and slid in a smother of snow into the creek-bed. Twenty-five yards ahead, behind the frozen willows that fringed the further bank, lay the desperado's barricade. With Millen beside him, Riddell clawed his way up the precipitous bank. As his forehead rose above the rim a menacing figure shot like a jack-in-a-box above the breastwork. CRASH! Splinters leapt from a tree beside the Sergeant's head.

"Jump!" he roared, sprawling down the bank in a shower of stones beyond the range of the murderous rifle fire. Two swift shots followed in quick succession and then—a sinister silence!

With fear clutching his heart, Riddell climbed the bank, defying Johnson's rifle. Suddenly, he emitted a gasp of horror. Inert upon the snow lay the outstretched body of "Spike" Millen, his *parka* torn and bloodstained. Ignoring the blood-crazed trapper, he seized the body of his comrade and dragged it to the ice.

"Is he . . . is he . . . ?" Verville's dry tongue refused to voice his fears.

"Dead!" answered the Sergeant grimly as he laid the body tenderly on the snow, his face cold as granite and lined with bitter hate. "We'll get that son-of-a-bitch yet—*or die in the attempt!*"

Stunned by the sudden and overwhelming tragedy, they sat disconsolately in the snow behind the protection of some rocks. "There's only one thing to do," rasped Riddell with grim determination. "And that is—stay right here and dog the heels of that miserable bloody rat across the creek. At the same time, keep out of range of his rifle. It would be suicide to attempt to rush that barricade. He could hold off a ruddy army on that bank there. I'll hike to Aklavic . . . report Millen's death, arrange for more supplies and ammunition, and send Hersey up from the base camp. *This* chase has just begun!"

Again UZK broadcast Inspector Eames' appeal for still more trappers and Indians to join in the manhunt, while the *moccasin telegraph*, the radio's prehistoric cousin, carried word to the oval lodges of the Loucheux and the squat cabins of the trappers.

"Get the Mad Trapper of Rat River!" became the slogan of the North.

From all directions, grim-faced men in fur-trimmed *parkas* hit the trail behind flying dog-teams for Aklavic.

From the outset, Eames had been faced with the one enormous handicap the North had yet to overcome—the difficulty of transporting bulky supplies of dog-feed and provisions long distances where there were no trails and the snow lay heavy and soft. Casting about in his mind for some means of conquering this, apparently, insurmountable obstacle, he had a sudden flash of inspiration. Why not have an aeroplane sent in from Edmonton? Not only would it assure ample supplies for the posse without these long, heart-breaking marches to and fro over snow-swept mountain and tundra but it would also permit both men and dogs to conserve their strength for a final dash to run this Johnson down. Again, if rifle-fire failed to dislodge him from his stronghold, it might be possible to bomb him from the air. So far, the Mounted Police had not become air-minded since Northern flying was still in the experimental stage but, still, it seemed the only solution to his problem. His mind made up, Eames sent his request crackling southward through the ether to "Punch" Dickins.

On Tuesday, February 2nd, 1932, Captain "Wop" May received from "Punch" Dickins, Superintendent of Canadian Airways at Edmonton, a wire requesting him to fly to Aklavic and join in the police hunt for Johnson. Dickins, himself, would fly to Fort McMurray with a Mounted Police officer and a supply of tear-gas bombs and transfer them to "Wop's" plane before he left.

Next morning "Punch" Dickins swooped down on the frozen Clearwater at Fort McMurray and transferred supplies, bombs and Constable Carter, who was replacing the unfortunate Millen, to the waiting plane. The enigmatic "Wop" crawled aboard, gave her the gun, and soon the plane was soaring down the Athabasca on her fifteen-hundred-mile flight through the thirty-five-below weather to Aklavic. Zooming low in the shelter of the Athabasca's fir-fringed bank, they roared northward till a blinding snow-storm grounded them at Fort Smith for the night.

Next day they were roaring north again, ploughing blindly through a howling blizzard, the earth beneath them completely blotted out. Dogged by bad weather, they reached Arctic Red River on Saturday, the 5th, and received word to meet Eames's posse at the junction of the Rat River and the Peel. But, though "Wop" circled the region for some time, not a living soul moved anywhere in that world of whiteness below them. Swinging the Bellanca around, he headed for Aklavic.

"Wop" awakened next morning to find Aklavic in the grip of another Arctic blizzard, and the Bellanca buried deep beneath a mountainous drift of snow. At noon there came a rift in the scudding clouds and the storm showed signs of abating. Armed with snow-shovels, Indians and Eskimos went to work with a will and dug the plane from its dazzling winding-sheet. Then, with Dr. Urquhart aboard, "Wop" zoomed into the frigid ether to resume his search for the patrol.

Not a sign of life did they see as they soared on through the snow-flurries. Below them, they sighted the V-shape junction of the Barrier and the Rat. Still not a living soul! The plane roared on. Suddenly Jack Bowen, the mechanic, gripped "Wop's" arm and pointed. Far below four diminutive figures, spread out in the snow, were creeping towards a clump of spruce.

Swooping down, "Wop" tried in vain to spot the fugitive but no other living being was to be seen. As the men stood up and signalled, May picked up his glasses and espied a single snowshoe-trail badly drifted, but showing up here and there on the wind-swept drifts. Dropping low, they followed the trail for five miles up the Barrier to find that the fugitive had doubled back on his tracks and swung from the river across a rock-ribbed ridge into a snow-filled valley, where the tracks struck westward towards the rugged range of mountains that separated the Mackenzie from the Yukon. There it petered out completely.

Zooming back to the Mounted Police camp, May dropped off Constable Carter, and learned that a storm had prevented Inspector Eames from meeting him at the mouth of the Rat on time.

"Better keep a close watch on that bird, Johnson," May warned the posse. "He's formed the habit of back-tracking over his trail. You're liable to run smack into him when you least expect to. If you do, *some-one's* going to be cold turkey!"

Next day, after an unsuccessful scouting trip, May dropped down at the police camp, picked up the frozen body of Constable Millen and flew it back to Aklavic.

Through the bitterly cold and boisterous weather peculiar to this mountainous region the search continued unabated, the Bellanca shuffling backwards and forwards—scouting ahead, and relaying supplies and dog-feed. On February 10th traces of Johnson's trail were discovered further up towards the mountains, with evidence that he was weakening.

"He's headed for Alaska," Eames told "Wop" a couple of days later. "I've wirelessed Anchorage, Alaska, to get word through to Constable May at Old Crow, warning him to be on the lookout in case Johnson gets across the divide. I'm thinking of withdrawing some of my men," he added. "It's too great a strain keeping them supplied with grub and dog-feed. Suppose you and Riddell take another scout across the divide, flying as low as possible?"

In a smother of snow, the Bellanca roared off again and headed towards the saw-toothed summit. Hardly had the plane disappeared from sight ere the crunch! crunch! of snowshoes caused everyone to tauten and grasp their weapons. Into the camp strode three strangers in fur *parkas* and *mukluks*. It was Constable May from Old Crow, accompanied by a huge, grey-haired giant—Frank Jackson—who had traded at La Pierre House for many years and knew the mountains better than any living white man, and Frank Hogg, another trapper. All were heavily armed, but not one of them had seen a sign of Johnson.

Suddenly there echoed on the frigid air the sharp crack of a dog-whip and the frightened yelps of huskies. Into the camp careened Peter Alexi, a Kutchin Indian from La Pierre House, flogging his dogs as though the devil was at his heels. "Johnson! Him cross'um mountains," came the guttural cry of the Indian before the team was properly halted. "Injuns—dey see 'im tracks on Bell Ribber two days 'go!"

All pressed around the excited Indian.

"Injuns," he continued, "dey all plenty scare. All leabe it dere traps an' come into de post!" A hunting party, he added breathlessly, had passed the place where Johnson's tracks were seen and had almost run upon him.

"That's our man, not a doubt about it!" Eames exclaimed with conviction. "He's made it across the divide. Now he's heading for Alaska."

A momentary flash of admiration appeared in his eyes. "He's sure *some* traveller. Ninety miles in three days, without dogs and through continuous blizzards. Now I think we've got him cornered!"

He turned to Hersey. "Better take Constable May, Hogg, Ethier and Jackson, along with Peter Alexi here and these two Indians," he ordered, "and make the passage through the mountains. I'll fly around with Riddell and Garlund and follow Johnson's trail before another blizzard drifts it over."

Soaring into the sky, "Wop" May picked up the snow-shoe tracks beyond La Pierre House and followed them around the looping bend of the icy Bell River for nearly thirty miles till they swung into the mouth of the Eagle River, only to be completely obliterated. Thousands upon thousands of caribou had beaten a hard-packed trail on the river-bottom and, taking advantage of this, Johnson had shed his snowshoes and trudged in their frozen tracks. But May had already observed a short-cut the posses could make to the mouth of the Eagle, and gain three days on their quarry.

Wednesday, the 17th, dawned grey and forbidding in a smother of snow and mist. Towards noon the fog lifted and "Wop," Constable May and Bowen soared off northward to the Eagle River. Soon they were soaring along at a hundred-and-twenty miles an hour, scrutinizing the rugged country and the white network of creeks and lakes below. Suddenly "Wop" stiffened. Far below, he discerned a black object on the ice in the centre of the frozen stream. Four hundred yards south of that, he observed half a dozen other specks spread out at the foot of the eastern cutbank. A movement near the opposite bank directed his gaze to two more dark figures silhouetted clearly against the dead white of the snow. From the east bank leapt a spear of orange flame, accompanied by a detonation. With a fierce thrill, he realized the significance of the scene. That lone black speck in the centre of the river was Johnson—the mad trapper! The other black specks were the posses, crouched along the river bank for cover. And that orange light was the flash of a rifle!

"*They're fighting!*" yelled Bowen. "*They're closing in on Johnson!*"

To the spiteful crack of Johnson's rifle and the rattle of answering gun-fire, "Wop" opened the throttle and zoomed in a wide circle above the icy battleground.

We came roaring down the river and once again I peered down at Johnson in his snow-trench. Then, as I circled over the posse, I saw a figure lying on a bedroll near the west bank and realized, with a sick feeling, that one of our party had been hit.

I circled back up-river, passing over the posse and Johnson. As I flew over the fugitive's lair it seemed as though he was lying in an unnatural position. Swinging back, I nosed the Bellanca down till our skis were tickling the snow. Johnson, I could plainly see as I flashed past, was lying face-down in the snow, his right arm out-flung, grasping his rifle. And I knew as I looked that he was dead. The Mounted Police had got their man. The chase was over!

I rocked the Bellanca back and forth to signal Johnson's death then landed on the river bottom and taxied over to where I'd seen the man lying on the bed-roll. "Who's hit?" I called out as Jack Bowen and I leapt from the machine. Sergeant Riddell was bending over the wounded man. "Sergeant Hersey!" he said.

"Badly?" I asked.

"I'm afraid so!" Riddell's face was grave. "He's wounded in the left knee, and the bullet may have gone up into his stomach!"

"Get him fixed up," I said, "and I'll fly him back to Aklavic."

While Sergeant Riddell was fixing Hersey up I strolled towards Johnson's lair, where the posse was gathering—staring at the dead man. As I joined the crowd Verville turned to me. "Just look at that face," he said. "Did you ever see anything like it?"

The man was lying, face-down, on the river and as I stooped over and saw him I got the worst shock I've ever had. For Johnson's lips were curled back from his teeth in the most terrible sneer I've ever seen on a man's face. The parchment-like skin over the cheek-bones was distorted by it, and his teeth glistened like an animal's through his days-old bristle of beard. It was the most awful grimace of hate I've ever seen—the hard-boiled, bitter hate of a man who knows he's trapped at last and has determined to take as many enemies as he can with him down that trail he knows he's going to hit. After that sneer I couldn't feel sorry for this man who lay dead in front of me. Instead, I was *glad* that he was dead. The world seemed a better and cleaner place without him.

Returning to the Bellanca we got Hersey in. He wasn't bleeding very much, and was fully conscious. Safely away, we got to Aklavic hospital in fifty minutes, where Dr. Urquhart cut his *parka* off him. Johnson's bullet had struck him in the left elbow, ploughed through his left knee, drilled his arm near the armpit then ripped through his body, piercing both lungs in the passing. The bullet was found just under the skin of the Sergeant's back. "He's in a very serious condition," the doctor told us, "but we may pull him through. Another half-hour would have finished him."

Johnson had crossed the divide over the highest peak, an elevation of over eight-thousand feet, a trip that must have been one long agony since, once above timberline, there was no firewood with which to kindle a campfire or warm himself and thaw out frozen food, and snow for drinking water. Yet the man had kept resolutely on, fighting his way through the teeth of the blizzards that swirled about him and plucked at his torn clothing.

The posse had come on him quite unexpectedly that morning. With Hersey in the lead, they were following his two days old trail when, around a fir-fringed point ahead, tramped a man on snowshoes—coming straight in their direction. Johnson back-tracking again—but with no idea his pursuers were so close! Snatching his rifle from his sled, Hersey opened fire. Slipping off his snowshoes, Johnson sprinted for the shelter of the bank, only to be driven back into the open by the barrage of Hersey's bullets. Like a cornered rat, he turned and blazed at his opponents. With a cry of agony, Hersey fell, writhing on the blood-stained ice. As Johnson fled for the opposite bank the rest of the patrol swung into action, hemming him into the centre of the river with a whistling hail of bullets. Fiercely, he flung himself down behind his pack on the naked ice and returned the fusillade. Though called on time and again to surrender, he kept up the fierce duel to the death. The first bullet hit his hip-pocket, causing the ammunition he carried there to explode and tear a gaping wound in his hip. There were wounds in the legs and back and shoulders, but the fatal bullet had passed through the small of his back, severing his spine. The condition of the desperado was terrible in the extreme. Thin to the point of emaciation, his feet, legs and hands had been frozen, and the only food inside his pack was *one lone squirrel.*

The frost-scarred, unshaven, ragged and weary patrol proceeded to search the sneering corpse. He was armed with a .30 Savage rifle, a .22 calibre rifle, a sawed-off .16-gauge shotgun and an ample supply of ammunition. In his bullet-riddled pack-sack were found two gold bridges from a man's mouth—which didn't fit his own; a razor, an axe, a leather poke containing a little gold dust; $2,500.00 in Canadian and United States banknotes, and some pearls, but not a scrap of paper that would give the slightest clue to his identity.

The Johnson case, the case that had shocked the entire North and thrilled the world, was closed, closed on a final note of tragedy. Yet, not entirely closed, for the true identity of the Mad Trapper of Rat River has yet to be discovered. From the very first, his swashbuckling attitude, his secrecy, and the large sum of money he carried secreted upon his person gave rise to the natural conclusion that he was a desperado who had come north to escape the clutch of the Law. His subsequent actions, his burning and unreasoning hatred of the Police, his fortified stronghold on the Rat, and his resolute resistance to the point of death all seemed to confirm the first impression. Yet, today, no more is known of Albert Johnson's true identity than the day "Spike" Millen questioned him at Fort McPherson and got coldly snubbed for his pains. True, scores of people have come forward as long-lost relatives to claim his money but, despite all this, the Mounted Police continue to report that "no progress has been made towards establishing his true identity."

1 3

THE TUNDRA
STRIKES BACK

With the advent of the aeroplane, and the blazing of new sky trails by "Punch" Dickins, Walter Gilbert, "Wop" May and other pioneer bush-pilots, the age-old methods of transportation, and the everyday life and routine of every trapper, trader, Indian, Eskimo and Mounted Policeman in the land, became entirely revolutionized. With the demonstration of the reliability of the plane, the North became definitely air-minded. Indians would casually hop aboard a plane to visit friends three or four hundred miles away; trappers scouted by plane for new hunting territory, or hired pilots to carry them and their grub-stakes to some erstwhile inaccessible spot, while aerial prospecting parties scoured the land from end to end.

It was the beginning of a new era, of a nation-wide assault upon the "frozen frontier." With the price of gold increased from twenty to thirty-five dollars an ounce, sourdoughs and *cheechakos* shouldered their packs again and hit for the tall timbers, to be followed by a surge of white adventurers, thrown out of gear by the Depression, who drifted northward in ever-increasing numbers hoping to recoup their losses by mastering the secrets that lay hidden beneath the granite bosom of the Great Lone Land.

Where, but a few short years before, had reigned naught but utter desolation there arose from the barren rocks, as though by the touch of a magic wand, thriving settlements and busy mining camps linked to the Outside by plane. On the shore of Great Bear Lake—only a decade before one of the loneliest spots on earth—thrived the bustling settlement of Port Radium, with its post office, stores, bank, houses and barracks, and aeroplanes flitting southward with loads of radium-bearing ore for processing at Port Hope. At lonely Yellowknife, where but a few years before I was glad to seek shelter from the Arctic cold in the squalid lodges of motley Dog-Ribs, another magic settlement was to arise, where gold-bricks would be poured from the wealth extracted from beneath its granite crust.

The entire North had thrown off the ancient, cramping shackles of the Fur Lords and gone modern. The aeroplane had demonstrated in the pursuit of the Mad Trapper its tremendous scope, swiftness and mobility over the slow-moving dog-team in policing the white wastes of the wilderness, a factor the new Commissioner of the Mounted Police was quick to take advantage of.[1] Thus, the air-borne Mountie was soon to be seen patrolling the northern reaches of their domain by a cruising aeroplane instead of plugging behind a tired team of refractory huskies, or "fish-burners" as the air pilots contemptuously dubbed the sleigh-dogs—whose regulation diet consisted entirely of fish.

Thanks to Prime Minister R.B. Bennett's questionable economics as a panacea for the Depression, the early summer of 1932 saw a further acquisition to the air-pilot strength of the quickly-expanding Canadian Airways. This occurred through the transfer of "Con" Farrell, Andy Cruickshank and Paul Calder from the Prairie Airmail, which they had pioneered, only to see it scrapped by the Conservative Government, to the Mackenzie River service. The Arctic air-mail was in need of extra relief pilots since this service, due to its many difficulties, required the most resourceful and capable pilots, and from this time on "Con" Farrell was destined to be closely linked with the other pioneer bush-fliers in a partnership of the skies.

Constantly on the go, "Con" seemed to pack more diverse episodes into his colourful career than fell to the lot of most bush-pilots. Amongst other things, he seemed fated never to be able to make Fort McMurray for the usual Christmas celebrations. One of his Christmases was spent in searching for a trapper whom the *moccasin telegraph* reported had fallen through the ice, losing both dogs and supplies. Since "Con" had deposited him in the Barren Lands in the fall he felt obligated to go and search for him. Starting from Fort McMurray, with his frozen Christmas turkey beside him in the cockpit, he located the trapper in the heart of the tundra, and reached Fort

1. During the summer of 1936 Air Commodore R. C. "Buss" Gordon, carried out a special transportation flight with the late Major General Sir James MacBrien, then Commissioner of the Royal Canadian Mounted Police, which carried them north to Great Bear Lake, the Coppermine, to Victoria Land, west to Aklavic and across the Rocky Mountain Divide to Fort Yukon, Alaska. By the time they had flown on to Dawson City, Lower Post and Fort Reliance, across the Barren Lands to Churchill, and headed back to Ottawa, this highly successful flight, covering a distance of some 14,000 miles, had been completed in the brief space of twenty-seven days—a journey that by old-time Mounted Police methods of dog-team, York boat and canoe, would have entailed years of arduous travel.—P.H.G.

Archie McMullen, left, and Con Farrell, ca. 1930.
Glenbow Archives NA-1258-39

Reliance with him on Christmas day, where he proceeded to cook the turkey and put on a celebration. In 1933 he set out on his usual Christmas mail trip. All went well till Christmas eve when a howling nor'wester forced him down on an un-named lake between Fort Good Hope and Arctic Red River, with the temperature at seventy-below zero—and no radio. In frigid loneliness, "Con" waited till the false dawn of the next day and flew blindly through the thickness until his unerring instinct brought him to Arctic Red River without mishap. In taking off, a cam-shaft snapped from the intense cold. When he arrived back at Fort McMurray thirty-eight days later, after repair parts had been flown in, he found, to his astonishment, that the social column of an Edmonton paper reported that he was "spending a leisurely holiday at the coast."

Around Christmas, 1934, it was "Con" who saved the lives of Andy Bahr, the Laplander, and his half-score of reindeer herders after the herd they had driven across the Rockies to Kittigazuit had stampeded and they were lost, along with most of their food supplies, in a sudden blizzard. A light dog-team fought its way eighty miles through the storm to Aklavic to summon help. The driver reached there just as "Con" was warming up his engine for the flight south. In a moment he exchanged his load of mail-sacks for a load of food, and reached Shingle Point as Andy and his party had almost abandoned hope.

On another occasion, while flying out Jack Stark, Gus DeSteffany, "Spud" Murphy and other northern trappers to their hunting grounds in the Barrens, "Con" and his engineer were carried far out of their course by a blizzard which left them stranded and out of gas in the vicinity of Snare Lake, one-hundred-and-sixty-five miles north-west of Fort Rae. Marooned here for thirteen days, they sat about the embers of their smoky campfire of stunted spruce and half-green willows, with flat stomachs, surveying their fast-disappearing rations of bannock and sow-belly and listening to the doleful wailing of the wind across the tundra, their thoughts better imagined than described. It was their good luck, however, to be located and rescued by another Northern flyer, Matt Berry, and his engineer, Frank Kelly.

But all was not near-tragedy and gloom. As "Con" was loading his big Junkers with express for Great Bear Lake the agent approached him with a grin.

"I've got a couple of extra passengers for you this morning," he chuckled, "but they're a little bit under the weather."

His disgust was decidedly vocal when he discovered that the "extra passengers" were a couple of odoriferous, train-sick pigs crated and consigned to Harry Reid of the Lake View Inn at Cameron Bay.

Promptly, word of the "distinguished passengers" passed from one radio operator to another all down the river until Cameron Bay was all set to appropriately celebrate their arrival.

Meanwhile, the August sun became hotter and hotter, and the pigs more and more air-sick. As "Con" taxied down-wind from Fort Rae he was preceded by an unmistakable aura of a far from well-kept farmyard.

At Cameron Bay, where a roistering gang of Northerners were celebrating Bear Lake's annual picnic, news of his pending arrival spread like wild-fire. The boys rose nobly to the occasion. A young and trusting medico, sublimely unconscious of the weird twists of Northern humour, was told that "Con" was carrying two passengers in urgent need of medical attention, and was advised to meet them at the landing, along with his nurse-wife.

By the time "Con" taxied in, his wrath was just below explosion point. As he skimmed in to the shore, he was faced by the local population—all ostentatiously holding their noses. This was too much! Leaping to his feet, "Con" proceeded to relieve his overwrought feelings in a blistering Northern blast until he suddenly spotted the nurse and doctor, patiently waiting to tend to the "ailing patients."

The dishevelled pigs, facetiously christened "Tillie" and "Mac," were delivered to their owner while "Con" aired himself and his feelings along the lake-shore. For months thereafter the easiest way to get his "goat" was to raise one's fingers and hold one's nose! In the February issue of the Canadian Airways *Bulletin* there appeared the following commentary:

Died at Cameron Bay, N.W.T., on December 27th, "Mac," beloved husband of "Tillie," of carbon monoxide poisoning. He was known as one-time protégé of Pilot C-o ("Porky") F-r-l, who had the honour of transporting both "Tillie" and "Mac" into the North, thus inaugurating an era of spare-ribs and pork chops in the Great Bear Lake mineral area.

With the onset of cold weather, the happy couple were transferred temporarily from their summer quarters near "Lake Shore Inn" to the Delco house at the same establishment. Here misfortune overtook them, and in the morning both were found overcome by gas fumes. Efforts to resuscitate "Tillie" proved successful, artificial respiration having been administered on the pool-table. But "Mac" had passed beyond this world of frost-bite, and the hope of multiple pork chops to come has thereby been temporarily blighted.

The North joins in sympathy with the bereaved "Tillie" and with her grief-stricken pilot friend.

Within a short time of his transfer from the Prairie Airmail to the Mackenzie, "Con" Farrell found himself engaged in the melancholy task of searching with "Wop" and Walter Gilbert for the missing plane piloted by Andy Cruickshank, and carrying two mechanics, Horace W. Torrie and engineer Henry James (Harry) King, on a flight from Great Bear Lake to the lonely Hudson's Bay Company's "meat post" at Fort Rae on the north-east arm of Great Slave Lake.

As this is written (reported Frederick Watt from Cameron Bay on July 4th), "Con" Farrell is gassing his Bellanca on the beach below prior to setting out on what may be the final search for Andy Cruickshank and his companions, now four days overdue. There is an air of ominous quiet hanging over the camp. Shortly before midnight yesterday we heard the familiar drone of an aeroplane engine coming up from the south. It brought every man in Cameron Bay out of his tent and sleeping-bag. It could only mean one thing, coming as it did in the middle of the night. Andy had been found, and the days of gnawing suspense were over.

When the two ships appeared in the sky to the south, one a

Fokker and one a Bellanca, there was a grateful shout of relief. It was taken as a matter of course it could only be "Wop" May, who had set out on the search two days before, and Andy, himself, returning to josh about the needless concern an ordinary forced landing had caused. At that moment the midnight sun broke through the brooding clouds and bathed the machine in an almost blinding flash of light. For an instant, too, letters were revealed . . . G-CASK. That was Walter Gilbert's craft which Andy flew. A new and sharper feeling of presentiment swept over Cameron Bay; the Bellanca wasn't "Wop's." It was flown by "Con" Farrell who, only that morning, had been at Fort Simpson, and who had run through vile weather to join the search! Farrell was not his usual chipper self when he landed. He explained he was very tired. He had seen on a hillside sixty miles north-west of Fort Rae what looked like a new cabin. "I felt pretty sick for a minute," he added. "It looked just like the yellow of a Fokker's crumpled wings with a dark patch in between that might have been the fusilage. It was probably only the peeled logs of a freshly-built cabin though."

"Con" produced his map on which he had marked the spot. "They're all old-timers in the bush," continued Farrell. "Chances are they're sitting there with a dead engine waiting for someone to come along and pick them up. I can just hear Andy and Hor Torrie kidding hell out of each other."

"Old-timers in the bush put up distress smoke-signals," suggested someone. "Did you see any?"

"No!" "Con" broke in with a worried frown. "That's what's been on my mind."

In ten minutes "Con" was heading back to examine that object that looked as though it might be a new cabin.

His premonition, however, proved to be only too true. The yellow object he had seen from the sky was the torn and crumpled remains of the missing plane, which had plunged into a low hillside on Mazenod Lake while flying through the thick mists that had impaired

"Wop's" flying that same day! Nearby lay the crushed bodies of Andy and his two companions, the first to meet with tragedy on the Mackenzie River service during the three years of Canadian Airways' operations.

Of the man who had flown 7,000 miles over the tundra during the historic MacAlpine search, only to meet a sudden and untimely death in those same Barrens, the Canadian Airways *Bulletin* had this to say:

To his friends his creed was revealed in a broad humanitarianism, as fitted one who in the great spaces of the North had communed with Nature in all her moods, had sifted the essentials, and freed his soul from the trammels of dogma.

Of unimpeachable integrity in business, fate treated him none too kindly in worldly affairs.

None doubted his ability as a northern pilot, a term which embodies qualities born of stern experience.

He loved the North, he loved flying and by none will he be more affectionately remembered than by those younger pilots who received their first instruction from him.

Exactly seven months later, "Wop" found himself committed to a similar melancholy duty in searching for the missing G-CATL with its pilot, the genial and irrepressible Paul B. Calder. In company with his engineer, Bill Nadin, an Air Force veteran from Crewe, England, they had headed out from Fort Rae for Cameron Bay on January 31st over the same tragic route that had proved fatal to Andy the previous July. Caught in a sudden blinding snowstorm, their wrecked and inciner-ated machine was finally discovered sprawled on the ice of Grouard Lake, ninety miles south of Cameron Bay. Storm-bound for a day, after flying Inspector Alan T. Belcher of the Mounted Police there from Cameron Bay to hold an inquest, "Wop" loaded the bodies of his two unfortunate friends into his plane and headed south for Edmonton, where full military honours were accorded Paul Calder. As the flag-draped coffin, on which reposed his R.C.A.F. cap and sword, was lowered to its rest a firing party from the 19th Alberta Dragoons fired three volleys, and the mournful strains of *The Last Post* rose in a final requiem to still another trail-blazer of the Arctic skies.

Hardly had the boys recovered from this disaster than word reached back from Norway House at the head of frozen Lake Winnipeg that Pilot W. A. "Bill" Spence, of Spence-McDonogh Air Transport, another veteran of the MacAlpine search, had met disaster at Moose Lake under almost identical conditions.

Meanwhile, the fact that Charlie McLeod and his party had succeeded in penetrating the Nahannie fastnesses, and coming out alive, seemed to break the spell that hovered over them and gave still another impetus to the search for the Lost McLeod Mine. Next to invade these fastnesses was Angus Hall of Myerthorpe, a brawny veteran of a score of gold-camps. Within a couple of miles of Dead Man's Valley he shouldered his pack and pushed ahead of his party, anxious to be the first to reach this elusive Eldorado—only to disappear as utterly as though the earth had swallowed him up.

More mysterious still was the fate of Martin Jorgensen. Lured by the same spell, he obtained an outfit from Poole Field of the Northern Trading Company at Fort Simpson and hit out for Dead Man's Valley. Months later a ragged Slavey Indian entered the fort and handed Poole a grease-stained note from Jorgensen urging him to follow, and saying he'd struck it rich. Hiring half-breed guides, Poole had followed on his trail. In the shadow of some nameless peak near the Flatt River he caught up with Martin at last. A headless body, struck down by some nameless and unknown hand!

Bill Powers, in whose cabin the writer had often camped on the Sickannie Chief River, was next to disappear. Leaving Fort Nelson, he, too, had hit the trail in search of the Lost McLeod Mine. When two years elapsed without word, the police set out to investigate. Beyond the spot where Jorgensen had met sudden and mysterious death they found the first evidence of disaster—skeletons of lynx and foxes in untended traps—and a sawed-off 30.30 rifle. Further up-stream they came upon the charred ruins of a log cabin with a blackened human skeleton amongst the debris and, in a nearby cache, untouched, a prospector's grub-stake identified as belonging to the missing Powers.

Again there was talk of murder!

Then big, strapping Bill Holmberg, well-known amongst the mining camps at Yellowknife and Great Bear Lake, had left Fort Simpson to disappear completely into the maw of the Nahannies without leaving a trace.

Despite this chain of disasters party after party now pushed their way by air towards the ill-fated Dead Man's Valley. They came from all directions. Even the wings of the American Eagle now soared over the snow-covered crags and depthless canyons until they, too, cast their shadows upon the slopes of the forbidden valley. Some parties zoomed up from the southward. Others came from the east, and still others from the west from Carcross in the Yukon. But one and all returned, defeated in their quest.

Word reaching Fort Simpson that still another boom was sending an overland party ploughing north from Edmonton kindled the flame anew. This time a number of Fort Simpson gold-seekers, determined to beat the overland party to it, felt that their star was in the ascendent when, in January, 1934, they managed to enlist "Wop" May's interest in the enterprise.

Mingling with Indians, river pilots and trappers, "Wop" heard rumours that had sent Jack Stannier on an abortive flight with Stan McMillan of the Mackenzie Air Services into Dead Man's Valley the previous year. They were to the effect that Father LeGuen at the Fort Providence mission had been a missionary at Fort Liard when the McLeod brothers had departed on their fatal expedition, and had in his possession an old map showing the location of the lost mine.

Flying to Fort Providence, "Wop" interviewed the aged priest. Together they rummaged through packages of papers, mildewed with age, and tied with moccasin thongs, until the priest unearthed a folded sheet inscribed in faded ink with the name of Willie McLeod. It was a rough map, stained with age and dampness, yet, clearly outlined was the route that Willie and Frank had followed in the summer of 1904, when he first discovered the gold. A serpentine line marked the course of the Flatt River while, to the westward, was a cross bearing the magic legend: "GOLD!"

Secrecy shrouded "Wop's" subsequent movements until the Edmonton *Journal* broke the silence with headlines announcing the disappearance of the noted bush-flier in the rugged region wherein so many gold-seekers had left their headless skeletons as a warning to others. Newspapermen had dubbed this region "Headless Valley" without stopping to realize that predators such as foxes, wolves and coyotes were probably responsible for the disappearance of these heads. A relief expedition, stated the *Journal,* consisting of Archie McMullen and engineer Frank Kelly had left Fort McMurray to search for the missing flier.

Meanwhile, "Wop" had headed towards the burnished summits of the Nahannies in company with prospectors Charlie Hansen and George Sibbitson, and mechanic Heuss. Blazing still another air-trail over the snow-capped peaks of evil omen he descended at last on the frozen surface of an unnamed lake considerably west of Dead Man's Valley. Leaving the plane, and following the route indicated on the map, the three men left Heuss to guard the plane while they scaled rock-walled hills and descended into mist-dimmed valleys. At last, they came upon a sight that sent the blood coursing through their veins. It was a half-frozen creek that, despite the cold, continued to bubble happily over a rock-bed fringed on either side with snow-laden willows. But what caused their eyes to widen after they'd examined an ancient camp-site were the snow-covered remains of rotting sluice-boxes, rusted gold-pans, and, beside them, picks and shovels—lying exactly as they had been thrown by the McLeod boys nearly thirty years before. Seizing a pan, Hansen washed off the corroded rust, filled it with black sand from the creekbed and whirred it with a gentle, rotating motion.

"Look!" his eyes were shining.

The dull gleam of gold met the pilot's eyes.

"I dunno whether this is the place or not," Hansen eyed the metal particles hopefully, "but there's gold here, right enough!"

Overdue for more than a week, "Wop" reached Fort Simpson to find that he'd already been given up for lost. But sensational reports of fabulously rich gold deposits in the rugged Nahannies, which heralded his return, were never destined to bear fruit. That they had located an old camp of the McLeod boys there was not a shadow of a doubt. That there was free-gold in small quantities was undeniable, but the mysterious gods of the Nahannies still withheld their secret, and the mother-lode that prospectors had searched for for thirty years seemed as far away as ever.

It was some years later that the writer learned from Charlie McLeod the final solution of the North's most intriguing murder mystery. Breaking the silence of years, Charlie told of the outcome of his search for his brother's killer. "I ran the man to earth," he said. "The murderer was my brother's partner, Wade. I found him going under an assumed name. For years he'd worked on one of the railroads, then on a lonely homestead—haunted, always, by the memory of his crime. Breaking under the strain, unable to stand it any longer, he climbed upon a haystack, set fire to it—then sent a bullet crashing into his head. I spoke to him many times," Charlie confided, "and he confessed everything. But, any vengeance I could have taken would have been nothing to the hell that he endured!"

It was shortly after this that Walter Winchell, on his Sunday night broadcast, announced that "Wop" May was missing in the country between Winnipeg and The Pas, and that his passenger was none other than the curvacious American fan-dancer, Faye Baker! Faye, it seemed, had decided to give the woman-hungry and "neglected" boys "up North" a few lessons in the higher arts, together with a proper appreciation of the female form divine. Arriving at The Pas by plane, she immediately got in wrong by showing a decided lack of appreciation of the musical efforts of the mooseskin-coated "Northern Lights Band" which had turned out to greet her with a fitting serenade. When Northerners proved unresponsive to Faye and her famous fan, which seemed disproportionate to the extent of human territory she wasn't trying too hard to cover, the young lady forthwith decided to fly back to Winnipeg and tell the world of her adventures in the Arctic.

It was when she and her pilot were four or five days overdue that Faye not only hit the Winnipeg headlines but the New York ones as well. All, however, was well when the plane turned up after a forced landing, and a not altogether too uncomfortable two or three days in a providentially-provided cabin in the woods, complete with fire-wood, food supplies and other essentials. From a Winnipeg hospital bed, where she reposed large-eyed and languid against a white pillow for the benefit of photographers and reporters, she told of her "hard-ships" in that lonely cabin. There was no caviar! No pate-de-fois gras! No fresh salmon or other foodstuffs and comforts *so* essential to a fan-dancer's well-being!

There were abroad many unkind souls who maintained the whole thing was a publicity stunt, and that the lady hadn't fared too badly in that well-stocked cabin.

Wrathfully, "Wop" declaimed all the honours accorded in Winchell's broadcast. He had merely been confused with Pilot *Bill* May of the North West Aero Marine Company of Winnipeg.

Note: As this book is being written arrangements are being made for a helicopter to invade the fast-nesses of Dead Man's Valley this summer (1954). "It will carry members of an Army map-making sur-vey team," reports the Calgary *Herald*, "one of nine teams who will fill in some of the blank spots on the map of Canada. Headless Valley, some 700 air miles northwest of Edmonton in the Northwest Territories, once had the legendary reputation of being a tropical valley populated with head-hunters. That myth since has been dispelled but map-makers still know little of that area. The survey team will be headed by G. A. Arnold of Ottawa, a civilian member of the Army survey establishment. Members of the Army establishment will work with the R.C.A.F. and civilian mapping agencies in extending Canada's defence mapping plan. The job won't be completed for several years."—P.H.G.

1 4

THE
NEARING NORTH

W hile the pioneer bush-pilots of Canadian Airways had been blazing new air-trails from the frontier to the Polar Sea there had been others who also shared the work of extending Canada's Frozen Frontier, one of whom was destined to loom high on the firmament of aerial pioneering.

A young Edmontonian, and subsequent winner of the McKee Trophy, Grant McConachie—now President of the Canadian Pacific Airlines—had received his flying tuition at the Edmonton and Northern Aero Club under the guidance of the veteran Maurice Burbidge. In 1931, Grant, like many another intrepid bush-flyer, proceeded to gain his experience the hard way—without hangars, flying fields or repair ships, "flying by the seat of his pants," to use the vernacular—in the rugged Mackenzie-Athabasca and Yukon regions. That fall he formed the Independent Airways with his uncle, Mr. Harry McConachie, and Princess Geletzine as shareholders, operating two Fokkers and a Moth. Two years later he formed the United Air Transport, in partnership with Barney Philips.

As recently as 1925 alternate air-routes to the Yukon had been considered by Canada's Civil Aviation authorities. These comprised a western route which would commence at Vancouver and follow, roughly, the coastline to Whitehorse. The eastern route would be linked with airports at Grande Prairie, Fort St. John and two additional airports in the heart of the almost untrodden fastnesses—at Fort Nelson, British Columbia, and Watson Lake, Yukon Territory.

The latter route, which avoided the mists, fogs and execrable flying weather of the coastal region, was surveyed in 1925 by order of the Hon. C. D. Howe, the choice being later confirmed by J. A. Wilson, head of the Civil Aviation Branch, after he had flown over every mile of it in 1936.

A pioneer air service had already been blazed by Grant McConachie over this rugged and almost unknown region of depthless muskegs, primeval forests and mighty peaks pierced only by the runways of the fox, the wolf and the lynx and the narrow snowshoe trails of fur-traders, trappers and nomad Indians. A region first explored by Robert Campbell, the Hudson's Bay trader, back in 1840; wherein the futile, million-dollar Charles E. Bedeaux Expedition with its shining limousines, Citreon tractors, uniformed wireless operator, pontoon rafts and other modern appurtenances came to grief in the summer of 1934. This occurred in the same year that McConachie and Ted Field, at the Government's request, surveyed an overland air route to the borders of Uncle Sam's forgotten step-child, Alaska. Considering the coastal route unsatisfactory, these two argonauts of the skies blazed a northwest passage by air east of the Rockies and through a low-lying pass to Whitehorse, then proceeded to organize the Yukon Southern Line. In this pioneering enterprise a bi-weekly contract was awarded them by Munitions Minister C. D. Howe and, by 1937, this service continued to fly in all weather without landing fields or other modern conveniences—Grant McConachie and his pilots putting their faith in the gods of the skies and pontoon floats along with a combination of infinite courage and optimism.

The first to inaugurate radio-compass flying in Northern Canada, he established radio-compass stations between Edmonton and Whitehorse for navigational purposes, which continued until the Department of Transport radio ranges were installed along the route.

Recognizing the advantages of wheel-equipped flying operations, Grant took the initiative in developing a chain of landing fields across northern British Columbia—at Fort St. John, Fort Nelson and Watson Lake. By 1939 his company was operating a weekly service from Vancouver to Whitehorse, connecting with air routes throughout the Yukon and Alaska; from Edmonton to the rapidly-growing Peace River region; from Prince George, in the forests of British Columbia, to Fort St. James on beautiful Stuart Lake, birthplace of British culture and traditions in New Caledonia; a monthly service from Prince George to lonely Fort McLeod and Finlay Forks at the headwaters of the Peace River, with side trips four times a year from Fort Nelson to Fort Liard; forever banishing from these lonely outposts the aloofness of former days.

Like all other aerial transportation companies, the Yukon Southern was no stranger to discouragement and frustration, and but for McConachie's superb handling of men, materials and finances, and the remarkable teamwork and co-operation from within, it is doubtful if it would have outgrown its swaddling clothes.

Meanwhile "Wop" May, who had contributed so much to the history of bush-flying, had been plagued by a private devil that rode with him in his lonely hours, a devil that constantly haunted him as he hunched over the controls of his speeding plane and watched the picturesque wilderness with its bejewelled lakes, its mighty rivers and endless marching columns of evergreens march past below. It was the haunting fear that blindness would, one day, terminate his flying career and write *finis* to all he had worked and striven for in matching his courage and wits against countless perils associated with wilderness flying.

Ever since that day back in Dayton, Ohio, when working as a mechanic for the National Cash Register Company, a vagrant and infinitesimal atom of steel transfixed his left eyeball, the fear had been with him; a fear that he kept secret from even his closest friends and which had been responsible for many dark hours when those unacquainted with the fact considered him, sometimes, morose and even unfriendly. To an air-pilot perfect eyesight was one of the utmost essentials, yet during the past two years gnawing pains in his eye made the veteran bush-pilot more than ever conscious of the fact that the damage he had hoped was only temporary had worsened.

Happily, in the fall of 1936, his problem was solved. From the headquarters of the Canadian Airways came word that "Punch" Dickins had been appointed Superintendent of Northern operations, and that "Wop" was to move, forthwith, to Edmonton and succeed "Punch" as Superintendent of the Mackenzie River district. Should failing eyesight now force him to relinquish the controls his time would be occupied with administrative duties, and if called upon to fly he could always requisition the services of one of the pilots.[1] The ubiquitous and resourceful "Con" Farrell, who seemed to be everywhere at once, and already knew the Northland like a book, was to take over "Wop's" duties as Chief Pilot.

1. "Wop's" eye was removed by a surgical operation the following year and replaced with a glass one.—P.H.G.

Hard on the heels of this announcement came a cable from London that His Majesty, King George VI had conferred upon both "Punch" Dickins and "Wop" May the distinction of the Order of the British Empire. But what, perhaps, gave "Wop" the most satisfaction was word that Louis Bourassa, the courageous mail courier who had forced his tired dog-team through snow-filled forests from Fort Vermilion to Peace River to send him on his first mercy flight with life-saving serum to stamp out the diphtheria epidemic at that isolated spot, had not been forgotten but had also been made a Member of the same exclusive Order.

The following year witnessed the extension of flying from the mainland and the Arctic Islands to the very shadow of the Pole following the epic trans-polar non-stop flight on July 12th, 1937, of the three Soviet pilots, Mikhael Gromoff, Andrew Yumasheff and Sergi Danilin, from Moscow across the roof of the world 6,262 miles to San Jacinto, California. When a party of Russian fliers disappeared in an attempt to repeat this epochal event, a Soviet appeal to the Canadian Government that a search be made for the missing men resulted in Sir Hubert Wilkins heading north to Point Barrow aboard the United States vessel, the *Guba*. To accompany him, Wilkins selected Al Cheesman who had piloted his Lockheed-Vega during his Antarctic expedition, another outstanding Canadian bush-pilot who had joined "Doc" Oaks' N.A.M.E.,[Northern Aerial Minerals Exploration Company] at Sioux Lookout back in 1927, and also done his share of flying with Western Canada Airways.

Using Point Barrow as a base, Wilkins and Cheesman combed the polar ice-fields with a Catalina flying-boat until freeze-up grounded them at Aklavic. With the approach of winter, they renewed their search of the shifting ice-pack, making wide sweeps to the very shadow of the Pole under the blue light of the full moon and the stars, in the same Lockheed-Electra plane that George Merrill and Lanby had used to fly the films of George VI's coronation from Great Britain to the United States. But, in that vast region of shifting ice and blizzard-swept Arctic islands their search for these infinitesimal human atoms was foredoomed to failure from the start.

By 1938 the shadow of Munich, of Chamberlain and his umbrella—the "undertaker from Birmingham," as he had been devastatingly dubbed by Winston Churchill—had swept to the farthest reaches of the North and bush-pilots who had been moulded in the flaming crucible of the First Great War had little doubt as to the shape of things to come.

Neither had the citizens of Alaska any doubt as to what was in store. Already the late, air-minded General Billy Mitchell had warned the White House that whatever power controlled Alaska in event of a future war would control the North Pacific, only to be broken for his pains, and be posthumously awarded the Congressional Medal by a conscience-stricken Congress when his forecast proved so unerringly correct.

As far back as fifty years before, F. H. Harriman, veteran United States railroad builder, envisaged a Canada-Alaska railroad to be linked with a projected Russian trans-Siberian railway by bridging, or tunnelling, the Bering Straits.

From time to time, the idea of an overland connection through British Columbia and the Yukon, to bring Alaska into closer relationship with the United States also made sporadic appearances before Congress, only to be shelved until Donald McDonald of Fairbanks definitely blocked out a proposed international highway on a map. Pursuing his idea with fiery zeal, he started a vigorous one-man crusade in 1928 for a road that would "link Panama with the Polar Sea," and painted glowing pictures in the *New York Times* of a wildly beautiful, primitive land with ancient totem-poles, vast caribou herds and flashing trout in tumbling cascades—two thousand miles of scenic wonders—that would foster greater friendship between the United States, Canada and Russia.

But in those good old days, when to speak of war was war-mongering and democracies seemed to think that the surest way to preserve peace was to blindly refuse to recognize the possibilities of war, the advocacy of the highway became bogged down and, by 1938, the progress had gone no further than the appointment of two new joint commissions to investigate costs and prospective routes.

In the summer of 1940 Alaska received a sudden and unnerving jolt when the paw of the unpredictable Russian Bear descended on Soviet-owned Big Diomede Island in the centre of the fifty-six mile Bering Straits separating this continent from Asia, and was reported to be establishing a large military air-base within a mile-and-a-half of the American-owned Little Diomede. For the first time, the realization was brought home to the American people that, instead of Russia and Asia being separated by the wide Pacific a scant fifty-six miles actually separated the two continents, and that—with only three hundred American soldiers stationed at Chilcoot—Alaska was wide open to enemy attack.

Warned by the potential threat of the Big Diomede, Congress and the War Department became galvanized into action, prepared to spend an initial $45,000,000 on Alaskan defences which soon catapulted to over $200,000,000, the first consignment of American troops disembarking on Alaskan soil from the *St. Michael* in the spring of 1940 to the hoarse cheers of the populace. By the summer of 1941, Anchorage, squatting in the shadow of saw-toothed crags already dotted with searchlights and anti-aircraft batteries, and flanked by Fort Richardson and the huge hangars of Elmdorf Airfield, found its population increased from three thousand to twenty thousand, most of them hectically engaged in these new defence projects.

At Fairbanks, the commercial capital, the army air base of Ladd Field had been established with underground quarters housing movies, clubs, canteens, living quarters and swimming pools, secure alike from Arctic blasts and enemy bombers.

At Sitka, with its ancient, green-domed Greek church, where "His Excellency" Baranof, the peasant autocrat, had ruled in all his glory, a submarine and air base was rapidly moving towards completion; whilst at Dutch Harbour, mid-way in the scimitar-like string of Aleutian Islands pointed like a dagger at the heart of Tokyo, a vast air and sea base was being rushed ahead. The only serious defect in the whole defence set-up was the fact that Alaska, for all its strategic importance, still lacked adequate connections with the arsenals of the United States. It was, in fact, like a front-line army without a supply line except for the slow and vulnerable sea route.

It was at this point that Canada was called upon to furnish the missing link, an aerial "Burma Road"—to become known as the Northwest Staging Route—that would provide the United States with the means of maintaining direct contact by plane.

Canada's readiness to co-operate was motivated perhaps by recognition of the plain and disturbing fact that Alaska was as much a frontier of Canada as the United States, and that an enemy established on Alaskan soil would have an uninterrupted run for bombing planes down the valleys of the Yukon and Mackenzie into the very heart of Western Canada. In consultation with Washington, officials of the Canadian Department of Transport drafted plans. What was needed, the Permanent Joint Defence Board decided, was a chain of fully-equipped airports with four-thousand-foot runways, radio, weather stations, and lighting facilities to guide night-flying pilots in all weather over a region of illimitable distances which would follow the route pioneered by Grant McConachie and Ted Field back in 1935. On December 18th, 1940, funds were released, the Canadian Government undertaking the plan at its own expense; contracts were let, and Homer Keith of Edmonton was appointed District Airways Engineer in charge of airport development at Grande Prairie, Fort St. John and Fort Nelson.

The first of these bush airports arose beside the bustling rural centre of Grande Prairie. Shipping material to the end-of-steel on the Edmonton-Dunvegan and British Columbia Railway which, in a last expiring convulsion, had reached Dawson Creek, the Tomlinson Construction Company hauled equipment to Fort St. John over a settlers' wagon-road that followed an old Indian pack-trail. There the old Beaver Indian camping grounds and race-course atop the thousand-foot plateau behind the old fort furnished another ideal site for a northern landing field.

But rearing a modern bush airport at Fort Nelson, a vital link in the new air-route across two thousand miles of almost uninhabited wilderness, broken only by the sleds and snowshoes of trappers and Indian hunters, presented quite a different problem. In March, 1941, tractor-trains with mechanical "cats" and cook-house cabooses, haul-ing seven-hundred-and-thirty tons, commenced to buck and bulldoze their way over the pioneer fur road the writer had blazed from Fort St. John to Fort Nelson back in 1925. After weeks of gruelling toil mas-tering matted spruce forests and bottomless muskegs the supplies were cached at the Sickannie Chief River, loaded onto scows, and soon the solitudes of Fort Nelson echoed to the tattoo of hammers, the jar-ring growl of drills and the rip of circular saws as a large airport arose beside the tepees of Chief Mattawa's wide-eyed Slavey tribesmen. Ere the geese were winging their way southward, Fort Nelson was linked to the outside world by a modern airport rushed to completion in record time.

Watson Lake, which boasted a solitary trapper's cabin, situated in a still more inaccessible section of the Yukon across the British Columbia border, was selected as the next in the chain of bush air-ports. Knock-down boats built at Vancouver were shipped by coastal vessel to Wrangle, Alaska, and transported up the swift-flowing Stikine to Telegraph Creek, famed jumping-off place for the big-game hunters and trappers. Hauled, seventy-five miles, over a sleigh road through primordial forest, they were reassembled at Dease Lake, loaded with equipment and towed up the Liard River to Lower Post, where a twenty-five mile portage road was cut to the chosen site, whence a sawmill and tractors had already been whisked through the air by plane.

Most northerly in this chain of Canadian air bases—later to be linked with the proposed Alaska Highway—was the one reared at Whitehorse, of gold-rush fame. Situated at the head of navigation on the two-thousand mile reaches of the mighty Yukon River, which empties into the Bering Sea at St. Michael, its long waterfront was lined with the red-paddled steamers: the *Whitehorse, Klondike, Nusaltin* and *Keeno*, that churn their way downstream to Dawson.

Here, in the storied land of "Soapy" Smith where straw-haired dance-hall girls mulcted *cheechakos* of their hard-earned gold dust, Archie McEachern and his crew of a hundred and thirty brawny helpers put the finishing touches to the last of these Canadian airports along the Northwest Staging Route.

To this modern air-base with all the latest aids to aerial navigation army bombers and planes of the Northern Airways and the Pan-American Airways soon were winging their way in ever increasing numbers, forerunners of the fleets of lend-lease bombers that were to roar up from the southward to be taken over by amazingly efficient Russian girl-pilots and crews at Fairbanks and be flown across the Bering Straits to blast the Huns from Stalingrad and the Dneiper, and finally bring Hirohito to his knees.

Hardly had the Northwest Staging Route been born, and American bombers commenced to wing their way to secret Alaskan bases, than the flaming fury of Nipponese aggression burst like a thunderbolt upon Pearl Harbor on that never-to-be-forgotten December 7th, 1941. In one fell swoop the worst fears of Alaskans and Pacific Coast citizens were realized in the holocaust that had descended on the United States Pacific Fleet, leaving mighty dreadnaughts an immobilized mass of twisted girders and displaced cannon, making the entire North Pacific vulnerable to carrier-based enemy planes.

For years Canadians had fondly cherished the illusion that their country was impregnable and unassailable, in case of war. That, separated by three thousand miles of ocean from bellicose Germany—and by the wide Pacific from Japan—they could treat with scorn the ravings of alleged war-mongers. But the new type of blitzkrieg, with airborne troops and screaming dive bombers bridging time and distance caused Canada to realize, with growing alarm, that what she had counted on as her surest protection—the isolation afforded by the vast, unoccupied reaches of her Northland—had, overnight, become an Achilles' heel, providing an undefended back door to flying squadrons bent on surprise attack. Japan's subsequent thrust at the Aleutian Islands, and the attack on Dutch Harbour, left no doubt as to her ultimate aim in dominating Alaska, and using it as a base to strike at the American continent.

Faced by this danger President Roosevelt was finally driven to stern measures to end the lengthy dispute over the route to be followed by a proposed Alaskan International Defence Highway to link threatened

Alaska with the United States, and on February 14th, 1942, a directive was issued to rush the work to a swift conclusion. At one-thirty on the bitterly cold morning of March 9th, with the thermometer hitting thirty below and a biting polar blizzard whipping the diminutive hamlet of Dawson Creek with a smother of drifting snow, the advance guard of the friendly invasion army, led by Colonel Robert D. Ingalls, stumbled from the "Sod-Busters' Express" to gaze in consternation at the world of whiteness broken only by a shadowy huddle of frame houses. The hundred-and-fifty-million-dollar Alaska Highway was, it was soon learned, to follow the exact route blazed by Grant McConachie and Ted Field, servicing the chain of airports already reared along the Northwest Staging Route.

Hardly had the first shipment of equipment for the Alaska Highway gotten under way than endless miles of steel pipe commenced to arrive at Fort McMurray for transportation by sternwheeler, *bateau* and winter road to Fort Norman, whence the oil discovered there was to be piped five hundred miles through the land of the mountain goat and grizzly to Whitehorse to furnish a back-door fuel supply to American planes, jeeps and trucks operating into Alaska. This one-hundred-and-thirty-million-dollar project had, in fact, been given its first initial springboard with Theo Link's Discovery Well at Fort Norman, the subsequent oil rush down-river and Gorman's historic attempt to introduce the first aeroplanes into the North, followed by the crash at Fort Simpson back in 1921 and the homeward flight with the "moose-glue" prop!

To survey and locate the Highway ahead of the construction troops, R. A. N. Johnston, forester in charge of aerial surveys and K. H. Siddall, chief location engineer of the Ontario Department of Highways, flew north with a special camera fitted to the plane, capable of taking miles of photos from eight thousand to ten thousand feet on seventy-five-foot rolls of film, ten inches wide. Flown nightly to Spokane, Washington, for development, they were brought back a couple of days later, placed side by side, subjected to stereoscopic examination and the shortest route selected with due consideration to muskegs and other impediments. Aerial reconnaisance had gone a long way since the days of the first pioneer bush pilots! As the work went on pilots of Alaska-bound bombers, winging their way through the skies, looked down on thin, pencil-like lines stretching tenuously through the dark evergreens that blanketed the land, drawing daily closer to each other.

Meanwhile, other sweeping changes, altering not only the complexion of this vast North country but the whole picture of aerial pioneering, had occurred when, on January 1st of this same year, most of the independent flying concerns, including the Yukon Southern, Ginger Coote Airways of Vancouver, the Mackenzie Services, Wings Airways of Winnipeg, Arrow Airways of The Pas, Manitoba, Starret Airways of Hudson, Ontario, and Quebec Airways and Dominion Skyways, most of them owing their origin to early bush-pilots, were taken over by Canadian Pacific Airlines—a branch of the world-wide Canadian Pacific transportation system. On the veteran Grant McConachie, then Assistant to the Vice President, fell the onerous task of welding these amalgamated airlines, scattered from the Atlantic to the Pacific, into a single operating unit with uniform standards of maintenance, communication, operations and equipment; and with them went the already famed and familiar emblem of the grey goose, together with many of the well-known bush pilots who had established bush flying the hard way.

Along the Northwest Staging Route, literally thousands of machines were flying from Edmonton to Alaska and on to Russia. Many of the American pilots were unaccustomed to the bitter cold, icing and other conditions associated with bush-flying in the North and as a result, "Wop" May, in charge of No. 2 Air Observer School in Edmonton, received constant calls to search for lost planes, and lost crews totally untrained to take care of themselves in the wilderness.

"We found one of these lost planes" "Wop" reported, "two miles east of Watson Lake, where it had made a forced landing on a bridge, killing pilot Hart of Minneapolis and co-pilot Kenneth W. Jones of Elira, Ohio. Determined to survive the tragic crash, the two remaining members of the party—Staff-Sergeant Edwin Wilvnski and Rupert Alexander—although suffering from broken legs, managed to crawl in slow, painful stages the two miles to Watson Lake through waist-deep snow, miraculously surviving for nineteen days in the mountainous and frigid bush country on emergency rations which had been fortunately carried on the plane. We rushed them to Edmonton by aeroplane, where they finally recovered."

It was this rescue that inspired "Wop" with the idea of training pararescue squads to operate throughout the thickly forested area of the North. "With the idea already perking in my mind," "Wop" recalled, "one of my boys—a former parachute jumper—kept needling me on the proposition so I decided to have him stage a demonstration—he did! He selected four besides himself to show what could be done, though I didn't learn till later that not one of them had ever jumped before! We kicked them out of a bomber over the airport. One chap landed on the wing of an aeroplane and went right through. The other guy landed on the American Officers' Mess, while another hit the runway flat-footed and jarred everything from his ankles to his wishbone. That wasn't so good, so we tried it over again. The next one landed all wrong. One lit on his 'fanny' on a pile of rock and bounced about six feet. I can hear him howling yet! By this time I got nervous and wondered what the devil would happen to these fellows if they were ever called upon to parachute into the bush. In utter disgust, I strolled over to relieve my feelings to some of the American officers looking on. One of them, a fine chap named Colonel Nitingale, promptly arranged to send some of these men to Missoula, Montana, where the U.S. Army was training smoke-jumpers—and the results were truly amazing."

Within a year the Edmonton *Journal* had the following significant remarks to make concerning the progress of the infant Search and Rescue Unit. "Wherever an aircraft flying over the Northwest Staging Route gets into difficulties which force it to land, or crash, in the wilderness of Northern Canada, means are now promptly available for locating it and dropping not only supplies, but R.C.A.F. men with extensive training in first-aid work and a knowledge of northern conditions at the scene of the mishap . . . The para-searchers of the division have received such specialized first-aid and medical training that they are even equipped to administer blood plasma if necessary. In addition, equipment has been designed by Air Force authorities to enable special medical kits and radios to be dropped from the air at the scene of the crash. R.C.A.F. officials believe that the existence of this unit has more than doubled the chances of survival of crews of aircraft forced down in districts hundreds of miles from other human help, or habitations."

The para-rescue squads, originating in the fertile mind of an erstwhile bush-pilot, were definitely an outstanding success, despite the first dubious "demonstration!"

Thanks to the hand of Mars, flying conditions throughout the North had now been completely metamorphosed by a chain of fully equipped airports with four thousand foot runways, radio and weather stations and lighting facilities to guide night-flying pilots in all weather across the heart of the wilderness of the Northwest. The Northwest Staging Route had been completed at a cost of $46,000,000, with flight-strips along the Alaska Highway costing an additional $6,000,000 and further flight-strips along the Mackenzie River route, first opened up by "Punch" Dickins, Walter Gilbert and "Wop" May.

The days when a pilot soared off from his base to be lost sight of till his return are now a thing of the past. No longer does he have to "fly by the seat of his pants," suck gallons of carbon monoxide into an empty stomach under a tattered tarp hangar after a meagre "Hudson's Bay breakfast" and, if he makes a crash landing in some isolated spot, have to wait hopefully for the intuition of a brother pilot to seek him out somewhere in the unmapped tundra. Today the pilot is in constant touch with landing fields, weather stations and bases, while scheduled operations have replaced the hazard and uncertainty of the early days of pioneer bush flying.

Looking back over the years since the first pioneer bush pilots challenged the age-old gods of the northern skies, one is constrained to paraphrase the words of that famous Statesman, Sir Winston Churchill: Never have so few done so much to conquer a vast and untamed wilderness as these early crusaders of the skies. There was Captain Gorman's return flight to civilization with his crippled Junkers and his famed "moose-glue" prop; "Wop" May's mercy flight through bitter cold and blinding blizzard in an open-cockpit plane to carry succour to the exiles of Fort Vermilion at the risk of his life; "Punch" Dickins' dauntless flight across the Barren Lands which had withstood man's assault from time immemorial; Pat Reid's casual conquest of the Northwest Passage by air; and Grant McConachie's blazing of the Northwest Staging Route that facilitated the rapid completion of the Alaska Highway and helped bring Hirohito to his knees; these and countless other heroic and outstanding efforts by Canada's pioneer bush-pilots to master the primeval wilderness and forever dispel its isolation, will always remain shining jewels in the story of Northern aviation and a challenge to generations to come.

About the Cover Art and Artist

The cover painting "Barrens Pioneer," by Canadian artist Graeme Shaw, captures a first in Canadian history. In the late summer of 1928, Clennel Haggerston "Punch" Dickins was chartered by Dominion Explorers of Toronto to investigate the possibility of prospecting the unexplored reaches of the Canadian north by air.

Punch took off from Baker Lake and headed toward Stony Rapids in his Fokker Super Universal floatplane G-CASK. The journey resulted in the first traversing of the Canadian barrens by an aviator.

Artist Graeme Shaw began showing his paintings in fine art galleries in 1971. His early work focused on West Coast imagery, but time spent living in the arctic and in the Canadian Rockies has also influenced his art. Both historical and imaginative works delving into exotic realms are included in Shaw's repertoire. His style is fluid, dictated by the demands of the images he seeks to create. After three decades of painting and dozens of one-man shows, Shaw's work can be found in Canadian, American, and international art collections.